FIGHTING THE FIGHT

"Drug overdoses are at epidemic levels across America. Fueled by the overuse and diversion of prescription opioids, addiction to heroin, fentanyl, and methamphetamines continues to spread and grow. No demographic is immune. We are losing people of all ages, and every income group, ethnicity and family situation. And no area of the country, from the biggest cities to the smallest towns, has escaped this scourge.

I applaud people like Alex Hoffman—parents who have lost children to this crisis and then have the courage to use their tragedy to help others avoid a tragedy of their own. The story of Shay Hoffman is becoming an all too familiar one: young people, full of promise, lost before they ever have a chance to live a full life.

I meet far too many parents, grandparents, brothers and sisters who have lost a loved one. Most of us have been touched in some way by similar tragedies. We all must endeavor to strengthen the fundamental building block of any successful society—our families. Legislators, educators and law enforcement, who have influence over policy, must strive to develop successful strategies to prevent this crisis from spreading, decaying our morals, and undermining the strength of our nation."

U.S. Senator Ron Johnson

"America has been remarkably slow to recognize the need to address our drug problem. With the opiate epidemic, death rates have been skyrocketing for more than 15 years, but only relatively recently has society as a whole finally acknowledged the need to act decisively and comprehensively. In three decades of law enforcement, I have never seen a greater public safety and public health crisis.

Our Last Day in Heaven shatters the myths that addiction only affects the so-called "bad people" or that we can just arrest our way out of it. It exposes this epidemic as the equal opportunity destroyer of lives it is. Alex Hoffmann will persuade you that no longer can we hide behind the mistaken belief that substance dependency is a sign of moral weakness or a character flaw. Alex makes the case that while there must be consequences for bad behavior, we must recognize addiction as a disease that must be treated compassionately and effectively if we are ever to free this epidemic's grip on our nation. He lays out a clear and compelling game plan for all of us.

Alex's story is one of courage and perseverance in the face of circumstances that would break the strongest of us. This book is an insightful and thought-provoking examination of the biggest challenge of our times. It provides answers to parents who are striving to understand the drugs that endanger their kids; guidance to public officials who must lead us out of this crisis; and a message of hope and healing to our neighbors who are struggling with addiction and can't see the light at the end of the tunnel.

We have much work ahead of us, but we have finally started to make progress. Much of that progress has come on the shoulders of people like Alex, who have turned their pain outward to issue an impassioned warning to us all, motivated solely by love and a desperate desire to spare others their ordeal. I am inspired by Alex's strength and am proud to call him my friend."

Brad Schimel; Attorney General, State of Wisconsin.

“Alex Hoffmann’s story is one of hope, courage, and commitment that flows from the very deepest well of a parent’s unconditional love for a child. He has successfully merged his great compassion and mission to honor his fallen son, Shay, with his skills as an executive to make a difference in the lives of others. He has fully dedicated himself—his talents, experience and knowledge—to a very practical and sustained fight against the scourge of addiction. Somehow in the face of all of the pain and suffering Alex has had to endure, he has stepped up and stepped out as a truly inspirational individual. His grief in loss has led to a lifetime dedicated to winning the war on addiction by battling against it proactively, with fervor, and on the very front lines of its existence.

It is very safe to say that every morning when Alex Hoffmann wakes and puts his two feet down on the floor, he immediately thinks of what he can do that day to advance the mission of eradicating the causes and consequences of addiction. He is motivated by the very deep, infinite love for his son, and regardless of the obstacle, he remains focused on that which can be accomplished, and not on what cannot. In the process, Alex has quietly met with and successfully advised our state’s top public officials, developing mutual trust and respect, and creating purpose in a battle against a soulless, faceless synthetic enemy that must be won.”

Michael Rogowski; Partner,
Husch Blackwell Law Offices, Madison, Wisconsin.

OUR LAST DAY IN HEAVEN

A Story of Tragedy, Loss, and Hope with Angels in the Midst

Alex Hoffmann

with Marla McKenna & Michael Nicloy

Foreword by John Nygren

Our Last Day in Heaven

A Story of Tragedy, Loss, and Hope with Angels in the Midst

Author: Alex Hoffmann

Contributing Authors: Marla McKenna, Michael Nicloy

Foreword: John Nygren

Editors: Reji Laberje, Kira Henschel

Cover Design and Interior Layout: Michael Nicloy

Our Last Day in Heaven

A Story of Tragedy, Loss, and Hope
with Angels in the Midst

ISBN: 978-1945907326

Published by Nico 11 Publishing & Design
www.nico11publishing.com

Be well read.

Quantity purchase requests can be emailed to:
mike@nico11publishing.com

FOREWORD

by John Nygren
Wisconsin State Representative

I first met Alex Hoffman shortly after the death of his son, Shay. A tragic story of course, but unfortunately Alex's story is not unique. In fact, it is all too common in a seemingly endless line of disastrous and destructive examples. These stories illustrate how addiction continues to have negative consequences on families and communities nationwide. These stories are the motivating factor behind his work in Wisconsin to fight this epidemic.

Like Alex, this issue recently became very real for my family. Now, more than ever, do I feel the catastrophic consequences of addiction. Wreckage left in the wake of addiction remains for friends and family members to pick up and put back together. But all is not lost, and from the darkness arises a new light, a new passion, and a new dedication to continue our fight, and our mission to eradicate addiction and substance abuse disorders.

When I was first elected to the Wisconsin Assembly in 2006, I would have never guessed I'd become a leader on substance abuse policy. My oldest daughter, Cassie, is a heroin addict. In 2013 I experienced something no parent would ever forget; their child on the bathroom floor, skin purple with a needle in her arm. It was in that moment that our lives changed forever. We were left to pick up the pieces the wrecking ball of addiction left on our bathroom floor.

Cassie was lucky. She survived her overdose, and by the hand of God she was given another chance at life. But the road has not been easy. In fact, it has been quite turbulent. We must constantly be reminded how fragile the road to recovery is. There is no easy way out.

In the face of absolute despair and helplessness, Alex did not collapse under the unbearable gravity of the tragedy that befell his family. Instead, he harnessed his pain and sorrow to transform his experiences into something good, and from his darkness arose a new passion and dedication to fight for the thousands of Shay's and Cassie's around the world.

As I read Alex's book, I was confronted with a flood of memories. I could feel the inner struggle facing Alex surrounding the death of his son. The questions a parent painfully must ask within themselves following such heartbreak can only be understood by those who have faced it themselves.

After facing the reality of Cassie's addiction, we used my role in the State Legislature to enact change at the state level. At the time of writing this in June of 2018, in five years 30 individual pieces of legislation aimed at combating the opioid epidemic facing the state have been signed into law. None of this would have been achieved without the countless partners and allies I have met and worked with. Alex was one of the first to join me in the trenches of this battle.

In 2013, we created the Heroin, Opiate, Prevention and Education (HOPE) Agenda with the goal of raising awareness and ending the epidemic ravaging our state. Alex reached out to me almost instantly to share his story and offer his experiences to help craft the original HOPE Agenda bills. Through Alex's leadership, we passed bills expanding access to Naloxone, also known as Narcan, a drug used to counteract opioid and heroin overdoses. We also expanded criminal immunity for people who overdose and those that are with them. This allows individuals to call for help and not have to contend with the possibility of prosecution. Our goal is to save lives.

Building off of the momentum of the original HOPE Agenda bills, Alex and I have continued to work to pass legislation expanding access to care and treatment to thousands throughout Wisconsin. Alex has played an instrumental role in making Wisconsin a national leader on substance abuse policy reform. And because of this, we are now seeing the fruits of our labor. Data released by the

Wisconsin Prescription Drug Monitoring Program is very promising. When comparing 2017 to 2016, Wisconsin saw 17.5 million fewer opioid doses dispensed. This represents a 12% decrease from the previous year. This 12% decrease helps close the door to future addiction and saves lives.

I want to thank Alex for sharing his story. Too often, stories of addiction are hidden behind the mask of stigma. Too often, our children are afraid to admit they need help. Too often, parents are afraid to admit there is a problem. Too often, when the time for help arrives, it's too late.

What follows is the raw, emotional story of a father whose life was turned upside down. A nightmare for all parents became a reality for him. There is nothing we can do to bring back those we have lost to addiction. But we can share our experiences in the hope that others will learn from what we have lived, and are still living.

Our Last Day in Heaven

To all of my angels, there are so many...

And to my children Nina, Harley, and Shay.
You are, all three, forever in my heart.

Missing you isn't the problem...

It's knowing that you're never coming back
that's killing me.

PROLOGUE

"Death is the not the greatest loss in life, the greatest loss is what dies inside of us while we live."
Unknown

I have an angel on my shoulder.

I've always believed this to be true.

I should be dead many times over. I should have quit on life just as often, but I somehow keep going...keep growing. It's that angel on my shoulder, looking after me to make sure I can fulfill my life's purpose.

In traditional Christian teachings of some churches, each person has his or her own personal guardian angel. That angel follows its person around to protect him or her from being hurt or making harmful choices. "Guardian Angels" started in the Bible and—within a hundred fifty years or so after the crucifixion—the celestial cherubs and spirits were already cultural icons. Somehow, across the centuries and millennia, there they have stayed. Angels were used in the literature of all the great, early novelists and playwrights; they remained a part of the teachings of many great philosophers; they became the subjects of legends and songs, and eventually appeared in movies and apparel and accessories.

Angels have stayed with humanity, guiding their charges to accomplish the unaccomplishable and survive the unsurvivable. Certainly, that's been the job of my angel. I don't know if my angel is fully equipped with a robe and halo, or if it strums away on its harp, but it's there. With my angel, I attempted to give up the bottle several times, so I know it's there. My angel has come to me in many forms over my lifetime. I know my angel is unseen, but I also know my angel has greeted me as a welcoming friend, an inmate, a corrections officer, a doctor, a brother, and, yes, an angel can even take the form of a lesson learned.

With my angel, I was cured of sickness…so I know it's there.

With my angel, I withstood divorce…so I know it's there.

With my angel, I recovered from bankruptcy…so I know it's there.

With my angel, I endured jail time…so I know it's there.

With my angel, I overcame addiction…so I know it's there.

With my angel, I survived tremendous loss…so I know it's there.

That day, though? The day I got that dreaded call from my older son, Harley? It didn't feel much like I had an angel in my midst on that day. That day I felt very alone.

I answered the call from Harley—

"Shay overdosed, and he's in a coma. It doesn't look good."

I can still remember that unending, fateful ride to the hospital:

I was numb.

I couldn't think.

I could hardly breathe.

It was like an out-of-body experience.

I felt helpless, sad, and confused…very alone. Where was my angel?

That's when my pleading with God began. It was then that I asked God to take me instead. We, as parents, say those words, and I can't speak for others but when I asked this of God, I was entirely at peace with my decision. I was prepared to go and nothing else mattered. How could this be happening? I was the dad. I was supposed to solve all my kids' problems, but I was powerless over this moment.

I felt like I was drowning along with Shay while he slipped away and finally went under. I couldn't grab onto shore and help him to dry land. Dry…the very concept from the mind of an alcoholic.

During my visits to Shay in the hospital, all of my problems became inconsequential. All that mattered was Shay and my family. I was helpless and my heart was broken. My spirit was broken too. Maybe that's why I couldn't sense my angel in those days.

Shay was in a coma for nearly five days, during which time specialists had confirmed he was clinically dead. The following day, when I returned to the hospital, I found out he had been taken off life support. He had passed on during the night…all alone. Shay's mom and I had talked about taking him off of life support, although we hadn't made a decision. As a parent, how do you even make a decision like that?

Shay passed in the night…alone.

I wasn't there.

He was alone when he died.

I wasn't there. I couldn't save him.

HE WAS ALONE.

I WASN'T THERE.

Perhaps, I died that day as well.

The hurt and pain I have experienced is not unlike many families across this country. It's a pain that doesn't localize, but envelops the body entirely. The feeling of loss when one's child is taken away is unimaginable and can't be described in words or on paper. Eventually, you accept the pain with the realization it will walk with you every day for the rest of your life. Then, one day, you take up your angel again and the weight gets shared. The pain subsides for maybe a moment or two when your angel offers relief; your faith is strengthened by hope rather than fear and pain. That's a feeling worth keeping but hard to hold onto.

A life was extinguished, my son Shay's life. This amazing young man had no hope of living his life's purpose. Shay was a child taken too soon...*my* child. I knew Shay's addiction would find its victory, and my son would find his defeat. But that wasn't like Shay, Shay was a winner. He was good at everything he did. He just couldn't win this battle. The addiction was his competitor, and it was stronger, faster, and even smarter. It eventually won; Shay lost his precious life.

You've heard the cliché: *losing a child is a parent's worst nightmare*. The thing is, it's not a cliché. It's the life I've lived, and the life I'm still living. I share this burden with my family as we cry over the devastating and unimaginable times, but do our best to remember the happy and joyful times when life was more like Heaven.

I titled this book *Our Last Day in Heaven* to play off of

a phrase people use when they post photos from their last day of vacation. I'm not sure if there is a particular point, but up to the time when Shay started having problems with drugs, life was idyllic. I had a great career that I loved, and I made more money than I needed. I had a loving family, and a pretty nice life. I didn't really buy anything for myself; I just really enjoyed taking care of my family. I loved being with my family. We went on a lot of family vacations all over the world and spent real quality time together.

There was a transition over a period of time, but it seemed like it was only a blink of an eye.

That was our last day in Heaven.

My life was pretty normal. It was actually pretty good ...until it wasn't. And through my journey I've always felt I had someone looking out for me, an angel in the midst, in good times and bad. That moment of being down one child, though, was lonely...we were once five and now we were four. And with the divorce, and as a single parent, it could be rationalized that now it was only three. But sometimes I felt like it was only one.

It was very lonely...*just as it had been for Shay in his last breaths.*

CHAPTER ONE
HEAVEN

A parent's joy is in the delight of his child's birth...
It is Heaven.

I have three children: Harley, Shay, and Nina. I count all my children as my biggest joys and blessings. They will always be the beautiful sunshine in my life.

The birth of a long-anticipated child is pure joy. What will he be like? Will he play football or perhaps be a Hall of Fame baseball player? Will he be prom king or will he excel in math? What music will he like? Will he share his artistic talent with the world? Will he make a difference? Shay was on course to be and do just that. I'm sure he would have made some kind of positive difference in this world. He succeeded at everything he attempted, and his future held unlimited possibilities.

Harley was the first. I was thirty-six years old when he was born in 1989. He was born with a cone head. I remember looking at him, lying there under the heat lamp...I must have looked worried, because the doctor came up right next to my face and said quietly, "Alex, it'll go away in a few minutes."

Of course, it did, and Harley was a strong, healthy baby boy.

Nina was just a doll, perfect health, a beautiful baby girl.

Shay was born December 22, 1990. He was one of the many blessings this life has given me.

Shay was born premature and was a mere four-and-a-half pounds when he entered this world. He was quite tiny, and we weren't sure he was going to make it. He had other ideas, though, and his strength persevered…then. Never could I have known what the next twenty-two years would serve up or the direction my life, or his, would take.

Shay was a beautiful boy, a sensitive soul. He grew into an amazing young man, athletic and smart, and he was so very kind. He was curious about everything and always charming. His list of talents grew feverishly every day, from painting, to drawing and sculpting, to playing the piano, to golfing, to running, to playing soccer. He just had an edge about him. He was a natural born talent. There wasn't much Shay couldn't do.

Memories of Shay

Remembering Shay is difficult at times. I just want to remember the good moments when Shay was full of love, energy, and fun. As a young boy, Shay reached for my hand many times. I liked that. I think back to cupping his hand as he held mine, thinking that he had really big paws for such a little guy.

As a young grade school student, Shay developed an unusual expertise with the claw machines often found in restaurants, bars, and bowling alleys. They were filled with colorful stuffed animals and fun for any thrill-seeking kid up to the challenge. To my knowledge, he never lost while playing one of those machines, and he often came home with an armful of stuffed animals and toys. He unselfishly shared them with his brother, sister, and countless friends. I watched him win many times, but I never could figure out how he did it, so I can't give away his secret.

When Shay was in middle school, he went over to a neighbor's house. While on the second story porch, Shay was greeted by their big, excited dog, and he was accidentally pushed into the skylight and fell through. I came home from work and my wife and daughter were attempting to put bandages on him. I could see how badly he was hurt, so I picked him up, while still in my work suit and tie, and rushed him to the hospital.

Halfway there, Shay looked up at me and asked, "Am I going to die, Dad?"

I replied, "Not today, Shay, not today."

He received twenty-two stitches. I still feel very uneasy when I think about that instance, knowing what happened that day. Shay clearly had an angel protecting him from the fall.

All of my children were great at sports; however, Shay was very fast and a bit of a risk-taker. He got more notoriety because of those attributes. I still remember him asking me a question. He and his brother played on the same team many times. Shay said he felt badly about all the attention he was getting because his brother wasn't.

Shay asked, "Dad, do you think Harley feels bad about it and should I quit the team so he doesn't feel bad? My brother is more important to me than the game."

Shay was unselfish and caring; he always put others before himself.

When the kids were in grade school, we took a family trip to Guadalajara, Mexico. Looking back, it maybe wasn't the best choice in vacation destinations. When we landed in the city, we were greeted by friends who went on to tell us, "If you get hit by another car, you should just keep driving. If you're arrested for any reason, contact this lawyer immediately. Don't let your children out of your sight because there are people who will steal them for money or pleasure."

What?? Why did we come to Guadalajara?

One of the nights we were there, we ventured out toward the city square and the fiesta. The mariachi band filled the streets with lively music...strings, guitars, accordions; instruments played in upbeat, rhythmic harmony. There were thousands of people that night, crowded together all in one place, dancing, singing, and laughing. The aroma of the Mexican cuisine and spices traveled through the warm night air tempting our taste buds while the brightness of the city lights overtook our sight and was somewhat blinding. There was so much going on; it was sensory overload.

All at once, we looked down and Shay was gone. *Why wasn't I holding his hand that night?* Overwhelming fear immediately set in; the world fell silent and dark. We only heard the echo of us calling his name, and in our minds everything and everyone else just disappeared. We frantically searched for Shay for what seemed like endless time. We saw Shay in every child we looked at and turned, but knew that child wasn't our Shay and that child was safe.

Where was he?

How could this happen?

He was right next to us the entire time.

Did someone take him?

Was he hurt?

Would we ever see Shay again?

God, where is he?

We were going crazy. I'm not actually sure how much time had passed but I think it was only around ten minutes. Then I felt a tug on my shirt. I turned and saw Shay looking up at me smiling that sweet grin I still hold in my mind to this day when I heard him say, "Hi Dad, I was just talking to people and looking around."

He was happy and just fine. We were complete wrecks. Losing a child is something you can never imagine before or after it happens, but we still had hope that time. Shay was the one who definitely had an angel in his midst that night.

We took another family vacation. This time we traveled to Puerto Vallarta, Mexico. To keep the kids occupied, we took them to a Go Kart track to relax and have some fun. There were tires stacked up along the track for safety, and the kids had lots of pads and helmets, and were nicely strapped in. I was still concerned about the dual engines on the Go Karts and the vehicles racing around the track at a pretty high speed. The first few laps seemed fine, and we thought we could relax. Then, all of a sudden, we saw tires on one side of the track flying through the air and dust circling like a storm. The stench of burnt rubber also filled the summer air. We could not see the track but soon Harley and Nina came racing around the corner. Everything looked okay...but where was Shay? Then out of nowhere, he appeared spinning around and heading toward the other Go Karts, traveling the wrong way on the track. What next? Never a dull moment with Shay! Eventually, with the help of the owners, we were able to get him safely turned around but it was a frightening moment in time that I continue to carry with me today.

Shay had no fear, and he displayed that confidence any chance he had. His angels worked overtime.

Another wonderful memory I hold close in my heart is when Shay and I went to see my favorite band, Boston, in concert at Summerfest on Milwaukee's lakefront. It may not have been his kind of music, but he went for me, and I'll always remember that night. Again, his selflessness and unconditional love was transparent in his effort to please me. Shay and I had a special connection, and that was a great father-son moment.

His academics were brilliant; he attended Marquette University High School in Milwaukee before moving to University Lake School in Hartland, Wisconsin. He graduated with honors and received a full scholarship to Milwaukee School of Engineering. After one year at MSOE, he transferred to Auburn University in Alabama. His future was bright, as if he held all of his dreams in his hands. Little did we know what he was hiding and what lay ahead.

Losing a child is something you
can never imagine,
before or after it happens...

CHAPTER TWO
ALL HELL BREAKS LOOSE

A parent's fear is in the loss of control of his child's life...
It is purgatory.

"You hear the voices too, don't you, Dad?" Shay asked me one day during a phone call. I felt my body go numb as I heard his words on the other end of the line but couldn't actually comprehend what he had just said. My son was hearing voices. Shay was battling more demons than we even knew. When I got off the phone, I cried. What happened next changed our lives completely and nothing was ever the same again.

We knew by 2005, Shay's freshman year in high school, that he was drinking beer and smoking marijuana. We discussed the dangers, and I wish that's as far as his addiction had taken him. We could have handled that.

By Shay's junior year in high school, we knew he was using some stronger "things," such as pills, because his behavior had changed along with his sleeping habits. We ran interference and worked with Shay the best we could. We tried to figure out what we could do and how we could help him.

Then the horrible day came when I saw Shay's drug usage with my own eyes. It started out as any other day. Shay often had friends over, and like all teenagers they retreated to their own corner of the world. At our home, that space was the basement. Our extra refrigerator was also in the basement and held what I needed. As I walked down the stairs, something I'd done hundreds of times before, I was horrified at seeing what was transpiring right in front of me. Truthfully, I will never get that vision out of my head. He knew we were all home upstairs, yet there they all were, his friends and my son. Shay, MY SON, was holding a rig, a spoon used as a burner to liquefy the drug, and a needle to inject the poison into his bloodstream. His arm was tied off with a large band, and he was shooting up right there in our home surrounded by his "friends."

I don't recall much else from that moment on. There was A LOT of screaming and yelling. We cleared everyone out; the other kids frantically ran up the stairs and bolted out of the house. This was beyond anything we had fathomed, worse than we had ever imagined. It was like getting punched in the gut. We knew we had to get Shay help immediately.

How could I not have recognized this earlier?

How could this have gotten so far?

We really didn't know that's what Shay was doing. We knew about the pot, the drinking, maybe pills. We knew it wasn't good, but we didn't know it was *that.* Not heroin. We didn't know *our* kid was doing *that* drug. Shay was addicted. A heroin addict can get hooked after one use, but we didn't know how many times Shay had used before I caught him in the basement that day. What we did know was that this was bigger than us, and fixing it was beyond our capability.

That's when we checked Shay into the Herrington Recovery Center in Oconomomwoc, Wisconsin. We knew he could get the help he needed there. He was falling apart.

We were falling apart. It was our only hope.

He would enter rehab a couple more times...and all of the times we took Shay to rehab, we never held an intervention for him, as is necessary for many families to do. He was always compliant when we took him to rehab. He wanted to get this demon off his back. He just couldn't...its hold was too strong.

Shay hid the signs of addiction and his use well; most addicts do. He was extremely smart and always ahead of the game. Nodding out is a common symptom of heroin usage when you start using too much...because you just don't know what mixture you're getting. A teenager nodding out while watching television is not unusual; that's pretty normal. It doesn't shout out, YOUR SON IS A HEROIN ADDICT. Shay told me he just couldn't sleep, so I really didn't think anything of it. He was up in the middle of the night painting most of the time, something he loved to do. I didn't recognize that as a problem or symptom of heroin use. None of us did.

How could I not recognize it?

How could I not see things?

Was there something more I could have done to save him?

I live with these questions every day.

I would guess he was using more than we thought. And I guess he was a really good actor. Even when you're an alcoholic, you can sort of act like you're not drunk or high... up to a point. Not that or anything else excuses me from missing it, though. It was just awful. I wouldn't wish it on my worst enemy.

After six months of rehabilitation at one of the best

recovery centers in the state, Shay came out clean...or so we thought. We didn't truly understand the recovery process back then so we didn't know what questions to ask, and he didn't offer much information. I do remember one beautiful summer day hanging out with him. We were outside playing Frisbee. It was sunny and bright. There were no clouds in the sky that day, and I didn't feel anything but hope for Shay and his future. We brought him home and with this new hope it was as if we could breathe again. But that hope was quickly suffocated. Shay began using again, and he just didn't stop. I can't say why he started again, other than heroin is an extremely addictive drug and thirty days, or even six months, in rehab just isn't enough time. Perhaps this too is when he began experiencing the onset of schizophrenia. He didn't understand that either... how could he? He medicated himself to feel normal. The horror grew worse.

As Shay developed a stronger addiction, his dealer demanded higher payments. He pawned my wedding ring and an expensive Omega watch I had. We had a very heartfelt talk about that over a year later, and I know in my heart that he was very sorry he did it. I told him that I forgave him and that I loved him.

That was just one more payment made though for one more hit. But it was never just one more time. As he used more heroin, he needed more money.

Out of options, Shay grabbed our big screen television from our basement living room. I was sitting on the couch in our main-floor living room, and suddenly, I caught a glimpse of Shay walking from the back yard, up from the basement to the sidewalk carrying our huge TV. My first thought was, *he's taking the TV...doesn't he think we'll notice it is missing?*

Of course we would miss it, but not in a material or monetary way. I mean we would notice that it was not there any longer. But he wasn't thinking like that; it was the drug and the addiction that was in control.

By the time I realized and accepted the reality of what I was seeing, he was running down the sidewalk; it was too late. I ran after him, but he escaped in a car that was his getaway, and they took off. I am pretty sure it was his dealer driving the car, and they were either going to sell the TV for money, or Shay just gave it to him as payment.

I was shocked, angry, saddened. I tried to rationalize it or make sense of it somehow...but nothing. He came back six or seven hours later, and we had an argument about what he did and that he was using again. But he just wasn't rational.

As I have learned more about addiction and have been working more and more with families of addicts, I have discovered that addicts do not seem remorseful about what they do or have done while they're using, or that they want/need to continue to use. But Shay was very remorseful about what he did and wanted to try to come up with a way to pay for the TV, my wedding ring, and the other things he stole...even though I knew he would never be able to. I honestly don't think he even realized that he stole the TV until he got back.

I don't think he was remorseful about getting more drugs—again, the drugs were in control—but I do think that he knew he did wrong by stealing from us to get those drugs.

Addiction once again claimed its victim. He was powerless. He had lost all control. It would only be a matter of time before he would lose his life.

Can heroin addiction be hidden? Yes, it can be hidden very well. We lived through the very convincing lies and secrets that tore us apart.

Addicts will do their best to hide the addiction from family and friends they are closest to. An addict's mind is not his or her own, and a user will cheat, steal, and lie to keep the secret. An addict also fears rehab because the thought of becoming clean is painful. The only hope for an addict is that someone will see the signs and offer help. But ultimately the addict has to *want* to get and stay clean.

With heroin use, anytime can be an overdose; it can be death. If you take as much as you took the last time, chances are you'll overdose. You're always chasing that very first high, which I've been told is like nothing else. If you take a break, it only hits you harder next time. On top of that, you never know what you're getting with heroin. Each new buy may be cut with a chemical to "stretch" its quantity, or the dealer may lace it with another drug to enhance the high, or just because he/she thinks it's funny. Every time you use, you are rolling the dice. That's what makes it so addicting and so deadly…like playing Russian roulette, but with no odds in your favor.

Shay was gambling with his life, and the cards were stacked against him. Heroin always has that hidden ace in the hole. Unless an addict can truly get and stay clean, heroin will always win.

<u>BE AWARE</u>

Common behaviors and signs of heroin usage and addiction include:

- Dry mouth
- Pale skin
- Pupil constriction
- Nodding off
- Slowed breathing
- Constipation/laxative usage
- Extreme weight loss
- Wearing long-sleeved attire even in warm weather to hide injection marks on arms
- Extended periods of sleeping due to numbing properties of opium
- Needles found in trash or empty soda cans
- Changes in behavior and personality, becoming more secretive
- Spoons with bent handles or burn marks
- Paper towel with brown smudge marks
- Mood swings: Incredibly happy to extreme sadness
- Signs of a suppressed immune system:
    - Chronic runny nose
    - Abscesses and skin infections
    - Scarred skin tissue
- Signs of schizophrenia: It is a scientific fact that heroine causes schizophrenia

CHAPTER THREE
MY BACKGROUND

What has happened to us in the past which was painful has a great deal to do with who we are today.

I was born into a prestigious family. My father was a doctor and my mother was a brilliant attorney and the youngest person to graduate from Marquette Law School in the shortest amount of time. She was fluent in Spanish, and, at one point, she was asked to be the United States Ambassador to Mexico…a pretty high honor. My grandfather was also a doctor—a surgeon—and the Founder and Chief of Staff of St. Francis Hospital in Milwaukee. Growing up, at least until I was in grade school when my dad bought a farm, we were well off, and I wanted for nothing. Even then, I had the best education money could buy, and I was on course to follow in my parents' footsteps, as was Shay to follow in mine.

Reyna, and my two good friends, Steve and Jeff.

My old friend from my youth, Jeff, was an extremely talented musician. One day he told me he was starting a rock 'n' roll band and wanted me to play bass guitar.

I said, "I don't play bass."

"I'll teach you," he informed me. And he did teach me, and quickly. So, we started our band. I played my new instrument, bass guitar. My brother played drums, and Jeff played guitar and was the lead singer. We called our band Reyna, which means "queen" in Egyptian.

My other good friend was Steve LaDue. He was one of my roommates when I was in college. He hung out with us, came to our gigs, and eventually became a de facto "roadie."

The band played at Milwaukee's Summerfest quite a few times, and also opened for some fairly big names like blues guitarist, Luther Allison. We got a recording contract with MCA Records in Los Angeles, which at the time was a very big outfit. We had the contract sent to us, and we were going to fly out to L.A. to meet our A & R agent, Sloan Rice, and sign the contract. The day before we left, I called Sloan to let him know that we were leaving the next day and that we'd see him then, etc., and I found out that he had been fired. He had been part of a pretty common and well known scheme by the record companies to pay off radio deejays to play their songs, only he had been paying those deejays with cocaine and other drugs, and who knows what else. He wasn't the only one doing that either, but he got busted for it.

When we got our recording contract, I offered our manager a separate management contract. He would have to pay us several hundred thousand dollars to sign with our band because he would be getting his cut from our MCA recording contract. He hated me for that, but at the time I thought it was a good idea, and it would have worked out well for him because we could have just fired him since we had gotten the recording contract ourselves without his involvement. He ended up signing, but refused to pay us. So not only did we not get our advance for our recording contract, we had to take our manager to court to get him to pay us. We hired Joe Balistrieri, son of Milwaukee Mafia boss Frank Balistrieri, as our attorney, but we lost the case.

Then it was back to square one for us, which really took the wind out of our sails; it was hard enough to get to where we were, but to start over was very deflating. The band just kind of faded away.

Jeff moved to Berkley, California for a few years. While he was out there, I went to visit him several times.

To give credit where credit is due, Jeff was a bit of a sociopath. He could talk to anyone, and say anything, and make it sound completely believable. Jeff had told me once in casual conversation that he had worked with psychologist Arthur Janov, the author of *The Primal Scream*, when he lived in Berkeley. Screaming was the rage in therapy at that time, and this Dr. Janov was known worldwide. At the same time, I was taking my first sociology course at University of Wisconsin-Milwaukee. We were still at the flower and beads stage in the early 1970s. The course grade was based on a project we individually came up with and had to submit to the professor for approval. Don't get ahead of me now...well, I came up with the great idea to bring Jeff in to speak because he had worked with the author of *The Primal Scream*. Surprisingly, the professor agreed.

The day of the speech, Jeff smoked about a half ounce of grass and said to me, "Hey can you get me the book, *The Primal Scream*?"

"Sure," I said, "but haven't you given this a lot of thought already? After all you worked with the guy."

In a moment of divine atonement, Jeff replied, "Well, I didn't really *work* with him...and I never read his book."

I started to sweat a little, but he spoke in the auditorium at the UW-Milwaukee to a packed house of around 1,000 students and professors. I got an "A" in the class, and I have no idea how he did it.

It was the early 1970s, and Jeff got his draft notice. He was picked number *four* (out of 300) in the draft lottery; a bad pick at the time, pretty much a guarantee that he would be going to be drafted and most likely be sent to the war in Vietnam. I got 300—that was a very good number; good enough to know that I wasn't going to have to go to war. I was in college at the time, and everyone our age got a draft registration notice and had to go through the lottery, but my number was so high that there wasn't even a need to talk about a college deferment.

Jeff was very worried. I'm not sure why I did it, but I told him not to worry, that Steve and I could get him out.

Steve and I worked on a plan to have Jeff flunk his physical, which was in two weeks. For those two weeks we kept him up around the clock utilizing stimulants, sugar, and a hodgepodge of other things. He was able to sleep thirty minutes here and there but after that we hounded him. On the day of his physical he was barely coherent. He acquired a twitch in his face and that lasted for months afterwards. The day of, with only a few hours to go, I had him drag his underwear through the fireplace and put shaving cream and ashes in his hair. Why not? He wasn't allowed to bathe for two weeks anyhow. When I dropped him off at the recruitment station, I told him he must convince them that he wants to join and he must never let on otherwise. I said this so often in the two weeks preceding the exam that I think at the end he started to believe it. He went in to get his physical while LaDue and I waited. After a few hours, he called, and we picked him up. He told us that during the physical and mental test he was not able to describe a hammer and could we help him with that. He said the recruiter came out and said, "Jeff we will not be drafting you, but Jeff, please get some help."

It took Jeff several weeks to get back to a semblance of normalcy.

I am really torn about that whole episode as I look back on it. I have a great respect for the United States as a country, the military and veterans, people who die or sustain life-altering injuries in the service of our country. But, at the same time, I truly believed that I was helping a friend who would have been detrimental to the military, his fellow soldiers, and himself, in that situation. To this day, I still have mixed feelings about that. It is not something I am completely proud of, and that guilt is something I carry with me. Maybe we were young and stupid; whatever the case, I feel I need to atone for what I did, although I knew then, as I still do now, that Jeff would not have made it through that experience.

My friend, Jeff was a unique guy with a big heart; I really thought a lot of him. I never met anyone like him before or since.

He was not in a good place for a long time. He struggled with mental illness, as well as other things, and passed away in 2004.

Steve was quite an interesting character as well. He was very intelligent. He read a lot, and retained information like no one I've ever known.

One night, we went out in Milwaukee. He drank too

much and was driving home on the freeway quite late at night. Cop came up, hit the lights, stopped, and walked up to the car.

Steve mumbled out, "It's zer a boblem ocifer? Wuzz I speedingk?"

The officer paused then said, "You were not speeding. You were going nine miles an hour. The speed limit is 50. By the way were you drinking tonight?" Steve told me that story when I came to bail him out of jail later that night.

One time, Steve had this brilliant idea to fly out to San Diego and pick up a suitcase full of marijuana and bring it back to Milwaukee on a train. I think somebody dropped a dime on him, because he got busted on the train right before it left. I flew out there to bail him out; he was scared as hell in the San Diego jail. While he was a prisoner, he worked on a crew with other prisoners fighting a wild fire that was going on in San Diego at the time. He told me about this aluminum bag they would give everyone who worked on the fire line, so that they could crawl into it if the fire were to overtake them and they would be saved. I told him that was pretty cool, and he said, "No, not really. It's common knowledge that it will not save you, but it will keep all your body parts intact."

Anyway, when he finally got out, we went up to Los Angeles to celebrate. We went out in Hollywood and we drank pretty hard. The next morning, I was up and at 'em in the hotel room, full of energy, bopping around and chatting away about the good time we had. Steve rolled over with his hair sticking up, and the first thing he said was, "Good morning, please extend the usual apologies to everyone."

Then he went back to try to sleep. I of course kept talking

and expressing what fun we would have that day. My friend finally got up and sat on the edge of the bed in his shorts. He rubbed his hands through his hair and said slowly, "Alex, I only have three brain cells left, and they're working really hard."

Steve died recently. He was a good guy and a good friend.

***

I graduated from the University of Wisconsin-Milwaukee in 1979 with honors and a Bachelor of Business Administration degree.

I was at that point in my life where I was done with college, and it was time to start a career. I wasn't really concerned about getting a job in my field. I happened to see an advertisement in the newspaper announcing the date, time, and place of the entrance exam to become a field agent for the Central Intelligence Agency (the people in the trenches, not analysts; these were the agents that got their hands dirty…I was applying to be a CIA "spook"). It piqued my curiosity, and I shrugged and thought, *Hey, I'll try it…*

I went to Madison and sat for the test, which was proctored by the Attorney General of Wisconsin. The test was mostly multiple choice. There was one essay question, I can't for the life of me remember what I wrote for that, but the Attorney General seemed impressed by it—in fact he told me it was one of the best responses he had ever read—and most of the questions involved geography, math, logic, and general multiple choice questions. But all of sudden there would be a question that was something to the effect of:

You are stationed in Germany and you are befriended by a couple that take you in and help you in some way (I can't remember exactly what the situation was, but bear in mind this was in the middle of the Cold War), *and you get a direct order to eliminate them. What do you do?*

It was also a multiple-choice question, and the choices were something like:

a. Call back and say "I'm not comfortable with that."

b. Call back and ask, "Are you sure you want me to kill them?"

c. Kill them.

d. Do not kill them.

I remember thinking that what they wanted me to say was that I would kill them, but I honestly cannot remember what my answer was.

After every ten or fifteen mundane questions, there would be a scenario like that. It was freaky. Toward the end of the day, I began thinking that this may not be the best career choice. But, I took it, I was proud of myself. Personally, I thought I would get in, although I'm not sure why I thought that. There I was, a long-haired rock 'n' roller, thinking, *I'm going to be a CIA field operative working in Europe or someplace in the middle of the Cold War…*

A few weeks after I took the exam, I told my dad I had gone to Madison and taken it. He said, "There's no way in hell you're going to work for the CIA. It's not going to happen, so just forget about it. They would just as soon kill you as look at you. You're not doing it."

He was adamant about it. I was pretty surprised at his reaction. He was a Goldwater conservative, voted for Nixon, former military officer, for the war in Vietnam (my friends and I were against the war). I didn't expect that response.

Now, the weird part was when I attempted to check on my results. We were told we would get an answer in two to four weeks. After a month, I hadn't heard. Another week went by, then another, and another. Finally, I called them. They looked for my results and told me that they had no record of me even taking the exam. I was shocked, and kind of aggravated. I ran scenarios through my head of my identity being stolen by the CIA, and being "disappeared." I'll never know for sure, but I suspect that my dad had something to do with my non-existence at Langley. At the time, due to his military service and political affiliations, he was connected with some government people and politicians, so it was very possible that he was able to get my exam and application incinerated; in fact, one of my friends shared the theory that my dad had "made a call."

So, I decided to find a job in my field of study, and started my first job in the finance world as a Commercial Finance Officer with a large bank in Milwaukee, and then transitioned into the real estate division as a Mortgage Loan Representative. I received my Master of Business Administration from Marquette University (also in Milwaukee) in 1985, and I had a few different jobs at several financial and mortgage institutions as Chief Executive Officer, Senior Vice President, Chief Operating Officer, Vice President, and President. I was doing extremely well, both financially for our family and in my finance career.

I got married in 1987, and welcomed my first child, Harley, in 1989. Shay was born in 1990, and my daughter, Nina, in 1992.

We went on many vacations like the aforementioned Mexico trips, both as a family, and a few of the times just my wife and I. We always had a great time traveling, seeing new places around our country and throughout the world.

For my fiftieth birthday, my wife surprised me with a trip to Egypt, to see the great pyramids. She drove us to the airport and told me on the way what we were doing. It was great. I obviously was not prepared to go there, so I didn't have any preconceived notions about seeing the pyramids; that wasn't something I had ever had any real intention of doing. I wasn't expecting some sort of existential experience at the Pyramids, but I am so glad that trip happened. Seeing these marvels had a real impact on me. We stayed in the only hotel that overlooked them. I would spend hours on the patio just gazing at their majesty. There is something about those things, I don't know if it is an energy or some sort of psychosis of mine, but there is something so weird, so fascinating about them. It's not just what you see, but also what you don't see. Perspective is totally screwed up. They are out in the middle of the desert, and there's very little to compare them with. They were so huge, it was just mesmerizing from that view. Even when we rode out on camel and horseback up close, it wasn't as dramatic as my view from that hotel. I can't really explain it, but something changed in me from that experience.

***

I have experienced a lot of tragedy in my life. Even in my younger years, before I hit rock bottom with my drinking/alcoholism, I faced many near-death experiences. Angels have always been in my midst and have protected me up to this point, and now I know why. My work here isn't done yet.

At age two, I suffered a hernia. My grandfather performed the surgery (which, at that time, was unethical and most likely illegal for one family member to operate on another), and at St. Francis Hospital, all of the nurses were nuns. One of them forgot to remove the mirror that was above the operating table. I remember lying on the operating table and seeing the mirror above me, I caught a glimpse of him making the incision.

I called out, “Grampa, you cut me.”

He let out a blue streak of expletives at that poor nun, who ran out of the operating room, crying.

He saved my life the first time.

Years passed as it should, with no other life-threatening incidents, with a couple exceptions. When I was around four or five, I tried to pull an icicle down from an overhang to give to a neighbor girl whom I was smitten with. I missed catching the falling icicle, and it hit me in the head, just avoiding my eye. It knocked me out and gave me a big gash on my forehead.

Then there was the time when one of my brothers gave me the brilliant idea to go down the stairs in our house in a cardboard box. It wouldn’t have been too bad, had it not been for the wall at the bottom of the stairs. My mom walked in through the front door to find me lying there unconscious.

My appendix burst when I was twelve years old. I remember lying on the cold kitchen floor trying to find relief as I was in so much pain. While on the gurney going to the operating room, the hospital’s priest gave me last rites when we were in the elevator. Again, I was saved by my grandfather…an angel.

In my grade-school years, I was a heavy kid and was

teased about my weight. My dad put me on a medication for weight control, which was a strong amphetamine. It worked; I did lose weight, but looking back, I think that probably wasn't the best for my brain chemistry. I learned that if you have a problem, all you need to do is just take a pill.

I did learn from that, however. When my son Harley was in second grade, around eight years old, attending a Catholic grade school on Milwaukee's East Side, his mother and I were called in to his school and his teacher told us that he was "hyperactive."

I asked, "What does *that* mean? Did he do something bad?"

She answered, "No, he can be a...distraction. We've all agreed he should be on Ritalin."

I looked at her and said, "I'll tell you right now, I'm not putting my son on Ritalin."

"What do you mean?" she asked.

I answered, "First of all, it's an amphetamine."

"But it will counteract the hyperactivity," she replied.

I countered, "Yes, in some cases it does, and some it does not. He's in second grade, for Pete's sake! He's a kid, it takes some kids longer to assimilate than others. This is not going to happen."

She said, "Mr. Hoffmann, we may ask you to remove him."

"I'll do it in a minute. I'll pull him out right now."

They backed off, and Harley turned out to be a great kid and a great student.

Why immediately put children on Ritalin instead of trying to help them work through whatever issues they are having? Help them learn how to adjust and sit still in the classroom. It's not unlike what I did. Instead of dealing with my problems, I decided to mask my problems by drinking alcohol. We see it with substance abuse, but we don't see it with kids. It's the same issue, you're not dealing with the problem, you're just masking it.

One of the reasons I feel strongly about this stems from an experience I had when I was on an airplane traveling to Hawaii with the boys, before Nina was born. There was a well-dressed Japanese businessman who was seated between my wife and me, and I was holding Harley. Harley was acting up, restless, and he got sick and threw up on that poor man. All over his nice suit. I was mortified.

I apologized all over the place to him, offering to pay for a new suit. I'll never forget what he said to me. He was completely calm and said, "No need to apologize. This is a child."

As he was cleaning off his suit, I offered to at least pay for the cleaning and he just said no, and that it was no big deal. He was very understanding and graceful. That is something that will stick with me for the rest of my life. It solidified my understanding that children do things like that sometimes, and neither they nor their parents should be blamed or punished for it. They are children, and they need to be understood.

Addiction and mental health awareness wasn't new to my family. I had been exposed to it before.

My mother had some mental health issues. One of my brothers, at about a year old, died in his crib, and the theory was her mental problems stemmed from never really recovering from that incident.

When I was fourteen, I came home from school one day, and my mother said to me, "I'm dying of cancer, and you can't tell anyone."

I was devastated. Honoring my mom's wishes, I didn't repeat her words to a soul. For about six months, I carried that with me, until one evening my family was at a neighborhood party with other families, and I was walking down our driveway, and I was crying about my mom. A neighbor girl, who was older than me, asked me why I was crying, and I told her that everyone was having so much fun and here was my mom, dying of cancer.

She said, "No. Your mother isn't dying of cancer. She has some mental problems. Your dad is having an affair; he's still taking care of your mom, but has offered her a divorce."

That really shocked me. Just like that, I went from my mother dying, to not dying but suffering mentally, learning of my dad's affair, and my parents facing divorce, all in one conversation with a neighbor.

My mom knew about the affair, but refused the divorce.

***

My dad was a very smart man. He was a doctor—and he was the patriarch of our family. He was always really good to me and the family. He and my mom went through a lot, mostly due to her mental disorder.

Doctors don't make the best business decisions. When I was in grade school, he decided to buy a farm in Hartford, Wisconsin, as an investment; not the best decision he ever made. We raised horses, veal cattle, sheep, and chickens. I grew up working on the farm.

In middle school, I worked at the farm before and after

school during the week, and on weekends, between feeding the animals at the farm, I worked at a drugstore in downtown Hartford. I went to University Lake School, a private school in Hartland, Wisconsin, in seventh grade, but I couldn't go there in eighth grade because the farm was going bankrupt.

My dad was a bit of a character. He served in the United States Navy, on a ship that sailed to and from Europe from the United States. He was the kind of guy who wanted to get things done. He pushed for life boats on the ship for every person the ship could hold. He pushed for morphine on the ship. He pushed hard for a second doctor to be on the ship. His theory was if he was injured or killed on the ship, the ship was screwed. He went so far as to fake his own death to prove the importance of having a second doctor on the ship, because there was no one else aboard who could declare him dead.

Apparently, he pulled a lot of stuff like that, and eventually received an honorable discharge, "For the good of the U.S. Navy."

Dad had a certain confidence in me…that I could handle adversity. He would tell me that he was never worried about me; that I was a survivor. He was concerned about my other siblings, but he always thought I could survive anything. He taught me to be strong and that I didn't need anyone.

When I was in high school, I came home from a date one night, and found out that, while I was out, Mom's appendix had burst, and she had died. My father came up to me and said, "Your mother is dead, and I'm about to fall apart. You need to handle everything."

What did I know about *handling everything?* I was *sixteen* years old, but that's how he saw me, what he thought of me. I didn't think about asking for help, I just had to do it. It clearly went through my mind, *Why am I doing this?* But there I was, leading the coroner into their bedroom where she lay dead on the floor with fluids all over from her burst appendix.

I think that created a sort of isolation within me mentally that got me into trouble later in life, and I think if I had gotten help earlier, I may have avoided some real hurt. I'm not blaming him. I think his intentions were good, I just never got out of the mindset that I didn't need help; I could handle anything because I was the strong one, the survivor.

***

When I was going to college, I would attend class during the day and then work second shift as an assistant lead supervisor at a cosmetics manufacturer in Milwaukee. We made lotions in huge two-story tanks. Once, one of my guys was working under one of the tanks, and he couldn't get the valve to open in order to pump the finished lotion into the shipping barrels. I got on my back to help. As I was working on it, the valve blew, and sprayed 200-degree water down the side of my head to my hip, causing third- degree burns. Later, the secretary at the plant told me, "Alex, up until that happened, I never heard you swear. You went from lying flat on your back to standing straight up and you were swearing a blue streak!"

I was in a lot of pain and went to the burn center at the local hospital. They bandaged me up and sent me home. Once I got home, I called my dad to tell him what happened.

"So, you're at the hospital, right?"

I said, "No, they sent me home."

"Give me that doctor's name."

I did, and I'm not sure what my dad said when he called that doctor, but he sure didn't have anything nice to say about him when he talked to me. He came and picked me up and took me to Hartford Hospital, where I was treated properly, and when I was released, I stayed at my dad's house. He told me that I had almost died from the mismanagement of the infection I contracted from the burn wounds. He treated me with the correct medication and pain-management drugs at his house. This was over Christmas break, and my dad had a couple of parties at his house for the holidays. I remember sitting blankly, not moving from my chair at the parties, and as everyone there was having a good time imbibing in Christmas cheer, my dad would come over with a syringe full of medication and bellow, "Well, time for your cocktail, son!"

***

In high school, I dated a girl named Barb, who at that time in my young life was my first love. She was an important part of my growing up. I thought the world of her, as did my family.

After high school, we went our separate ways, as many couples do. We both got married and started families. We had been in touch off and on through the years, although we didn't see each other.

One night at around three in the morning, I got a call from another mutual friend who simply stated over the phone, "Barb's dead."

Her husband was a licensed pilot, and a good one too (I also have my pilot's license, so I know a good pilot when I see one). They were returning from vacation on a private plane, and she got out of the plane and walked into the propeller and was decapitated. It was a shock to hear. It was difficult to digest. She had a young daughter, and a lot of anguish came over me for her daughter and her husband too. It was sad and difficult to wrap my head around, especially at her funeral, when I offered my condolences to her older sister, and she said, "We're sorry for *you*." That was how close Barb and I were. Her family understood that and really felt badly for me.

***

I think some of these traumatic incidents when I was younger have affected me in my adult years. I boxed things in. I built walls around myself, and that caused me to take on everything myself, and not share it, not talk about it, not get counseling. Incidents like seeing my mother die when I was sixteen and having to do all of the work my dad couldn't do, as well as many of the traumatic events that happened to me over the course of my life, created a hole in me that drove me to fill it with alcohol. I adjusted to things poorly. I realized many years after Mom died that I had issues with attachment. I was afraid to fall in love for fear that the person I loved would die. That had an effect on my adult life, and there were so many holes that I needed to fill artificially.

In my marriage, work issues, my drinking, problems at home…I was smart enough to know I should have gotten help, instead of thinking that I could handle all of it just like I always had. But I did not. Instead, I just isolated myself and bottled up all my anxieties, and eventually started to self-medicate with alcohol. I've always thought counseling is a good idea, because any kind of introspection can't hurt you; it's actually good for you. I just never did it until it was too late. Eventually I did get help, but it was after I nuked my life.

CHAPTER FOUR
MY ADDICTION

A man's escape is in the bottle,
that particular man being me...

All of my children grew up wanting for nothing, just as I had; a beautiful home in a well-established neighborhood, cars, vacations, you name it, we had it. Life was good. You could say it was like Heaven.

Then, in 2007, the mortgage crisis hit and the market became volatile. There was financial panic and turmoil around the world. And that's when the personal panic and turmoil hit close to home and struck the Hoffmann household even more.

That's when all hell broke loose.

The company I worked for closed the mortgage division I had created and was president of a few years earlier. It was done, and I was out of work with the attached stigma of being an aging, over-qualified bank president. How would I ever find a job in that high-level capacity again? Where could I go? This was my career, my success, my legacy that I was leaving to my children. This was what I knew and was good at.

With no job, there was obviously no income, and it had been a significantly high income. My wife didn't need to work, in fact; I made a good living for all of us. But, even before all this happened, we were spending a lot of money, so much money that eventually we were going to have to tap into my retirement fund. We were also paying for Shay's rehabilitation and all of his attorney fees. When there's addiction in the home, there is dysfunction throughout the entire family. Emotions are high; nerves are raw, and there's no time for judgment, but that's exactly what happens, and that's what transpired in our home. The blame got thrown around and there was immense conflict between spouses, parents, siblings, and addict. Ultimately, we weren't trying to punish the person who transformed into an addict before our very eyes...we were trying to save his life. But when the wheels are coming off the household, everything—and I mean everything—goes bad.

Once you've lived that kind of lifestyle, one that affords you every luxury, it's hard to break the spending pattern and habits. The money disappears, but the desires for the good life don't. The mental efforts were exhausting and caused the communication to break down and even more blame was tossed around. Money flew out of our bank account as if we had won the lottery; cars continued to be purchased; vacations continued to be booked...because "everyone does it."

We were basically trying to keep up with the Joneses.

I told my wife, "This is not gonna work."

There was no job in sight. The spending needed to stop!

To make matters worse, four months after my job loss,

I stopped eating. I felt extreme thirst all the time. I was completely sluggish. My new disposition was mistaken for laziness. But I knew something wasn't right. I needed to see a doctor. Another month passed, and the doctor almost immediately admitted me to the hospital. The diagnosis was clear; I had diabetes. I was experiencing all of the symptoms. I just didn't know it.

Sluggish
Extreme thirst
No appetite

Six months after the job loss, we dipped into the IRAs. I didn't know how long my unemployment was going to last, and we needed the cash, not only to pay the bills but to continue with the lifestyle...so many needless expenses were being incurred.

Around the eighth month, I still had no job*, but on the bright side I had diabetes,* I thought sarcastically. Shay was desperately spiraling out of control with his drug use. I was running interference on that and what seemed like everything else, and it all went to hell in a hand basket... going from bad to worse.

No job
No money
Over-spending
Panic
High blood pressure
High cholesterol
Diabetes
Constant friction
Marriage derailment
Family derailment

My dad always said I could handle adversity. I didn't need anyone. But there was one thing I did need...*alcohol.*

So, I started drinking. Another six months went by before I really hit rock bottom. At that time, I felt no angel. I felt no presence of God. I only knew I felt better when I drank... because then I felt nothing, and that felt good. So, I drank whenever I wanted. Drinking escalated my functionality. I was better, faster, and stronger with alcohol. Spinning out of control, I actually felt more in control than I had in a long time. I felt free.

It's interesting how I couldn't stop drinking and really didn't want to stop drinking. Yet, I overcame an addiction to prescription Vicodin, after I survived a neck injury due to slipping on the ice while holding and protecting Shay from the fall (yes, that happened too). I had an MRI about a year after that, because the pain got worse, and it showed two herniated discs in my neck. My doctor prescribed Vicodin with an extra Ibuprofen to manage the pain and said I'd probably be on it for the rest of my life. I was not happy about that idea. He continued to prescribe the painkiller every month. I was also trying to manage my pain through exercising, acupuncture, and chiropractic, and that therapy was working, so I stopped taking the Vicodin. Every time I stopped taking them I would get physically sick; I was going through withdrawal. I told my doctor that I wanted off the painkiller, and he admitted me to the hospital for several days to detox. I got off of the painkiller relatively easily, considering the detox, especially in comparison to how difficult it was for me to quit drinking.

I felt like I was having a sort of out-of-body experience; watching a movie of my life with the script written and directed for me and without my consent; it was like I was in a car chase and the brake line was cut and I'm pushing and pushing on the brakes and about to fly right off a cliff.

It all kind of ran together; Shay's addiction, my addiction, the family falling apart, I went to jail for DUI (Driving Under the Influence), the divorce, the bankruptcy, my diabetes...I was medicating myself with alcohol to cope, to just get through. Every jagged piece had its very own unique place in the thousand-piece puzzle, but that puzzle was never going to be whole again. I had lost myself completely. It was a bad couple of years.

While in therapy sometime later, the psychiatrist, after hearing my story to that point, told me that I had a mental breakdown; there was just too much coming at me and I didn't have enough arms to hold all the packages.

Finally, after hitting rock bottom, I must have heard that still small voice inside my head—or maybe it was my angel—screaming at me to get help. God had plans for me...big plans. I just didn't know it at the time. I heard the angel's scream only as a whisper though, as it had so much noise to break through in my head. Even then it was so hard to hear.

Eventually, I started rehab. My first rehab was at the Herrington Recovery Center, the same place that Shay was for his first time through rehab. I walked the same halls as Shay did during his rehab and sat in the same rooms. I talked to counselors who remembered him. Although, I'm sure Shay's thoughts of recovery and my own mirrored each other, it was a learning curve because while going through a similar experience I was also trying to better understand what he went through. It was sad, lonely, and introspective as I reflected on my life.

A few months after I left Harrington, I started drinking again, and eventually went back into rehab, this time at a different facility in Appleton, Wisconsin. I met a young lady named Cassy, who was about twenty years younger than I was, and we became good friends. Our relationship was in no way physical; we had a sort of father-daughter relationship. Over the few months that I was there, we had become very close. She checked out of the rehab facility and moved back into her house in Madison, and we would talk about me visiting when I got out. I was still in that rehab center when I got the news that she had died of an overdose. That was a very traumatic event for me. I really was heartbroken.

And in the same pretense as yin verses yang and that life can't be all good or all bad, I was served with divorce papers.

I wasn't surprised.

Another six months went by and my wife declared *"innocent spouse."* She claimed she wasn't responsible for the IRA penalties we acquired while married. I was then called by a representative who asked me, "What do you have to say, Alex?"

I asked what was said so I could respond but the caller wouldn't tell me. I'm not exactly sure who she was but she made it sound like she was from the federal government. I didn't know how to respond because I didn't know what my wife was saying. I did ask again what was said so I could attempt to respond accordingly, but she would not tell me anything. But it really didn't matter. I was assigned nearly $250,000 in tax penalties.

That hurt.

What a crushing blow.

Divorce can take everything from you.

Not only can it destroy you financially, it can drain you emotionally. It can take your children. It can take your integrity. It can take your life. My brain was like mush. I wasn't thinking clearly. I couldn't even afford an attorney.

During the court hearing, the judge said, "Let's talk in chambers."

My wife's attorney argued, "Alex is a drunk and doesn't deserve anything."

You start to question everything. Is she right? My wife was someone I loved, the mother of my children, my partner. Did I not deserve anything? Yes, I made mistakes, but so did she. But I was still a man, a husband, a father, a human being. I did deserve more.

The judge asked me, "Are you an alcoholic? How are you?"

That was sobering…someone who actually cared. She showed compassion.

I replied, "I haven't had a drink in six months."

"Good for you! You've made some bad decisions, but you can move forward," he said reassuringly.

Then she asked with apparent concern, "Mr. Hoffmann, I can't represent you, but are you sure you don't want to ask for alimony from your wife?"

I don't remember specifically what I said, but ultimately I didn't ask for alimony. For the sake of my children, I wanted to put this to rest so everyone was taken care of. I didn't want to rock the boat because the kids were still reeling from everything that had happened. I also didn't want to screw anyone over. I really wanted them to be able to assimilate back into normalcy of life. The last thing I was thinking of was taking care of myself or how fairly I was being treated. I had screwed things up, and it was time to pay my penance.

Now I know that was a mistake. I should have looked after myself as well as the kids. When I give advice to people getting divorced, I tell them: "Go for everything you legally deserve, don't be a jerk, but just to be fair to yourself, because you can always step back and renegotiate, or cut a check later or change it."

I didn't get anything out of the divorce except the bills. Like my drinking, I needed to put it behind me and move on, move forward. My drinking came with more high costs though, in the form of four DUIs in two years—two before the divorce and two after—and I had to serve time in jail for my crimes.

***

On a slightly lighter note…

When I was arrested for the second time for DUI and was being brought into the city jail, the arresting officer spoke into the intercom for us to be let in for processing,

"I'm bringing in the DUI arrest from earlier."

The voice on the other end of the intercom said, "Do you have the good DUI or the bad one?"

I was relieved to hear him say, "It's gonna be a great weekend, I got the good one! He's been compliant, very polite, always saying 'thank you' and 'yes sir.'"

"Oh, good," she replied. "I guess the other guy was a real pain."

So that gave me a glimmer of hope that at least I was the "good" DUI.

CHAPTER FIVE

MY NEW HOME

A man's consequences are in his choices...

Homeless to jail.

Toward the end of my drinking career, after all the efforts to help me were exhausted by my family and friends, my drinking problem hit a breaking point. I was staying at my brother's house while I was waiting for my court date to be convicted of my multiple DUI charges, and, one night, we decided that I couldn't—and shouldn't—continue to live there. I was drunk again, and my brother drove me to a makeshift detox area in the inner city. I had no place to stay. I had no place to live. But I didn't want to be a burden to him. This center, my temporary *home* for a couple of nights, was a cold cinder block room with about twenty-five cots puzzled together to fit inside this small area. It was dirty, dark, and frightening.

I couldn't help but think, like many times before:

How did I get here?

How could I let my life get this bad?

I still remember a young black man who must have recognized that I was nervous and out of my element. He was also one of the residents in this unwelcoming "home *not* sweet home." This place was unsafe for everyone who occupied it.

He told me not to worry. He would watch out for me.

Why would he do this for me?

Why me?

Why was this person I didn't even know watching out for me?

Was he an angel sent by God to protect me?

He moved my cot to the corner, and he positioned his cot as a shield, warding off anyone who had ill intentions to bother me.

I tried to sleep but it was nearly impossible. He said he'd help me, but I didn't know him. How could I trust him? How could I trust anyone in this place? I was uncomfortable, and it was cold. The mattress was cold. The metal bars it laid on were cold. The odor in the air was that of mold. There was coughing and sneezing and talking and yelling. It wasn't quiet. But those sounds weren't any louder than the noises in my head. They were constant, I couldn't silent them even though I tried. I sensed fear and I sensed mine to be the greatest. *How did I get here?* I was a broken record as I played the same song and dance over and over in my head. If I survived the night, something had to change. *I had to change*.

To my dismay, I made it through the night without any trouble. I thanked this man—this friend—extensively. He was a very kind soul and expected nothing in return. He was simply a generous human being helping another in his time of dire need. To this day, I don't even know who he was or why he showed me such compassion. I wish I could thank him again as I believe he may have saved my life.

He was an angel, but this wasn't the only angel in human form that saved me. More were to come, and I would need more saving.

A couple of days later, I had detoxed, and I needed to find new quarters. My brother picked me up in the evening and took me to the only place he could find for me...the Milwaukee Mission. We walked in and both immediately turned a distinct shade of pale. It was awful—worse than the detox center I had just left.

I was scared. I could NOT stay there. I'd rather have been on the streets. My brother had already called the Salvation Army, one county over from Milwaukee, but they had no room. We went to a coffee shop across the street from the mission and discussed my rapidly decreasing options. We kept coming back to the mission as the only choice for me. I said a prayer, and then asked my brother to call the Salvation Army shelter one more time to see if there was anything they could do to help me. My angel looked after me once again. The person he spoke with said they just had a space open.

I cannot say enough good things about The Salvation Army. They require the people who stay in the shelters to develop a plan to do something with their lives within thirty days. You could only be at the shelter from 5 p.m. until 9 a.m. the next morning. Then you had to go out and do something. That was good for me, because it gave me a sense of purpose and something to do. I won't lie, I was experiencing extreme loneliness at this time, and much of the time it was very difficult for me to fill those hours. I would often go to the library to read and look for work on the computer. I would also go to the Al-Anon Club after it opened and spend some time there. It can be pretty grim when you have no help and no sense of direction. It was pretty difficult for a few months to adjust my mindset to not going to work at the bank with dozens of employees. I was adjusting to a new life; I had to bury my old life and build a new mindset.

I worked in the Salvation Army kitchen and as a bell ringer during the holidays, and I ended up staying about six weeks.

When I first started bell ringing, a seasoned bell ringer gave me some advice: to get women to put more money in the bucket, "Tell them what great shoes they have. They will give more money."

One day I was working at a store when a well-to-do, well-dressed, attractive woman came in. I saw her moving toward the door on her way to leave, she tossed some change into the bucket, and I remembered the advice, and thought, *that's right! Remember to compliment her shoes*! Well, she was wearing boots, and as she walked toward her car, and shouted after her, "HEY! NICE BOOTS!!"

She looked at me in terror, as if I had just pulled a knife on her.

I yelled back, "BOOTS*... BOOTS*!"

Another lady walking past her looked at her and said, "He did say *boots*."

Once I left the shelter, I found a friend I could stay with

for a couple of months until my court date, when I was convicted of my DUI and sent to Huber, a corrections facility.

***

"Huber Law" is a Wisconsin statute that provides jail facilities in counties across the state. Huber facilities are jail, make no mistake, but they are for any person sentenced to a county jail, who may be granted "work release," the privilege of leaving the jail to work at a job. There are many other circumstances that qualify a county inmate to receive the privilege of the Huber Law, such as job training, education, medical treatment or counseling, etc. But for me, it was work release.

In Huber, an inmate may only work up to 55 hours per week, three or more days per week, and must be in the jail for an entire day, one day per week. Inmates are also required to either have health insurance or prove they are covered under their employer's Workers Compensation, and provide a pay stub to the jail staff. They are also required to pay a fee to cover expenses incurred by the county to house them.

The terms "jail," "work release," and "Huber" are all synonymous.

I worked two jobs: I started as a dishwasher and moved up to cook at a restaurant called Crossroads, and I was a cashier and in maintenance at a golf driving range.

Life is like photography,
you use the negatives to develop.

CHAPTER SIX

MEMORIES (AND SOME WISDOM) FROM JAIL

A man's wisdom is in his experiences...

good and bad.

I have been out of jail for some time now, but thoughts from my time there come back to me quite often. I journaled regularly while at Huber, and I also started noticing things that piqued my interest, and I began writing them down. I learned a lot while I was in jail—I just wish I had learned it in a different way.

My journaling was also a way I could reflect on my survival that was consistent with the faith and unseen strength I held in every situation. My faith grew as I read *The Bible* front to back three times during my incarceration.

There are lots of stories, some more brief than others, and some entries were short thoughts I titled: "Wisdom From Jail." It should be noted that in most of those entries, I use the word "wisdom" sarcastically.

The following journal entry is by far the most haunting and frightening for me:

I had to go to Milwaukee County for court, to face my third DUI charge. [Keep in mind I was already on "work release" and serving time in Washington County Jail for my second DUI.]. *While in court, the judge covered several things: When I received my first DUI in Milwaukee County, and the second in a suburb of Milwaukee, they were fairly close together, timewise. The two cities, Milwaukee and Glendale, did not know about the other DUI because I had not been convicted of either one at the time. My very high-priced attorney timed the court dates so both municipalities thought they were a first DUI, and both were settled that way. When I got the third, it triggered a review, and each municipality discovered the other's DUI. So the second DUI had to be tried again. The attorney—now court appointed, because I was broke—argued "Double Jeopardy," which the judge threw out because it was a municipal violation, not a criminal violation. I had to be booked again for the second and third offenses. The judge ordered this while I was at court, even though I'd been booked previously. I was in Huber in Washington County, so booking should have only taken twenty minutes. That was no problem. I was then shackled and taken to the Milwaukee County Jail at eleven o'clock in the morning. While in jail, I was shackled to a wall with gang bangers and heard some pretty interesting conversations. The other inmates were all in the standard issue orange jumpsuits. I was in street clothes, and more than one of those guys remarked that I looked like I could be their lawyer.*

My heart raced as I sat there, knowing full well this was not where I was supposed to be.

I tried to explain, but no one would listen. After an hour, I was taken to a room with seventy-five other inmates waiting to be booked. Meanwhile, my brother waited for me the entire time. While in this room my fear elevated…more waiting in a space I shouldn't be in the first place. I minded my own business. I withstood long eye contact. Then, a very large black man was looking at me laughing.

Eventually staring at me, he said, "Hey, you're a virgin, aren't you?"

I said, "Yeah it's my first time!"

The man laughed even louder, and we began to converse. He continued, "Hey, you look like you could be any one of our lawyers!"

We became friends during the continued stay. The head guard of this group screamed out occasionally that we had no rights and better behave because we didn't deserve to live. The day continued. Guards took breaks and chatted around, and we waited. There was talk if it went too long we'd have to go upstairs to jail and wait until morning to get booked. What about Huber, my other jail? I thought.

Around 6:00 pm, we got what was distantly called a meal of baloney and bread. Some inmates used them to sit on because the benches were so hard. Worried that I would be considered AWOL and Washington County would issue an arrest warrant, I asked the Jamaican head guard, (sort of the Idi Amin of Milwaukee County Jail), if he could call the Washington County Jail and let them know what was happening. Idi, as

I now referred to him affectionately, said, "Well you technically are not under arrest so you don't get any call, not even to your mama."

My mother had been dead for over twenty years so that didn't concern me. However, I was puzzled why law enforcement agencies did not want to help each other. Idi was the ruler of this jail and apparently no one was going to invade his country no matter what. The cleaning crew was coming through so we had to all get locked up in cells. Twenty to a cell designed for six. It was one way to get to know your neighbors. The crew cleaned up the sandwiches everyone sat on.

About 7:30 pm, a guard looked kindly on me and said, "Well I'll squeeze you in here to get booked."

Ok, tough day but the nightmare is about to end, I thought. Now, the judge said I would be released right after booking was complete. It was 8:30 pm, I had been there since 11 that morning, and I was ready to go. Due to some miscommunication, I was told I had to stay overnight at the jail upstairs until my situation was sorted out. Given a blanket and some soup, three other hopeless souls and I headed for the elevator. As the elevator opened, I was told to go back and sit down. I was not going upstairs. Thank God, they finally figured it out. I could get out of here and my brother could take me back to Washington County Huber Facility Jail. Well at 9:30 pm, I was told they had not worked out the problem and I had to go to the House of Corrections in another city until they figured everything out.

"Can't I just go back to my other jail please?" I asked, trying not to appear like I was pleading. I was chained up and put on a bus with thirty other men

going in the opposite direction of my Huber jail. "The boys" and I finally got to the house at 11:30 pm, and at 11:55 pm, we got the introduction speech that loosely consisted of…if you get in a fight you go into solitary. You will wear pink underwear and a jump suit. You will eat nutraloaf exclusively. Nutraloaf: jail cuisine; a protein brick, gummy and greasy in texture, brown or grey color. And don't be surprised if there are cockroaches in it. It tastes so grotesque, you won't eat it. It was a good weight loss program.

By 1:30 am, I was in the bunk area with seventy other guys. There was another central guard who sat up high in a big desk. A red line about ten feet away from the desk separated us. We are told if we crossed that line we would be sent to solitary with our pink underwear and nutraloaf. I explained to the guard from a distance of about twelve feet away why I wasn't supposed to be there. This new guard was no Idi Amin, but he didn't seem to care anymore about my situation any more than Idi did.

I decided to go to bed, especially since the lights were out already. I wouldn't want to wake my fellow sleeping beauties. Incidentally, I was told by a guard earlier that no one in this room had been arrested for murder, but there's no guarantee that they had not murdered someone previously. Pleasant dreams. Sleep tight, with one eye open. Everyone up at 5:30 am for something loosely referred to as breakfast. I sat down alone at a table with my gruel. Within minutes two very large fellas sat down next to me. One of the gents remarked—utilizing his keen powers of observation—he had noticed I was a new guy. Thankfully the guy didn't say "nude guy."

The curious hombre went on to explain that new guys are supposed to give veterans of the jail their food. A treat, as he affectionately referred to it. Thinking about the nutraloaf and pink underwear along with never leaving this God-forsaken place, I said nothing. If there's going to be a fight, I was going to take the hit and go to the floor.

After a few minutes the poor man's Hulk Hogan said, "Well the new guy at least has to sing us a song."

I was not able to come up with a rendition of 'Melancholy Baby' that appealed to him, and with a very dry mouth by now, said nothing. Look out floor, here I come. Just then, the guard, Idi Amin's cousin, called out my name.

I walked up to the red line, not crossing it, and said, "Good morning officer."

Idi's next of kin replied, "Good morning, inmate," just in case I forgot my situation in life.

Then this wonderful cousin of Uganda's Supreme leader said, "What the hell are you doing here?"

I replied "That's what I've been asking all of you for the last twenty-four hours....SIR!!"

The guard asked if I could get a ride to the golf range I worked at before the restaurant and get the hell out of here. I dutifully called my brother. I finally left the Milwaukee jail and went "home" (Washington County Jail). There were some very touching moments when I said goodbye to my breakfast buddies.

Journal Entry:

A young black inmate with wild afro hair sat down to talk to me. I was humbled, and found this to be odd because he didn't pay much attention to me except when he would pick on me at times. He spoke to me about problems he was having with the jail and work. I gave him some advice and told him it would work out and I'd pray for him. Just then the corrections officer came to talk to him about his problem. When he came back I told him I prayed for him and he said, "It worked out. Thanks for your prayers."

I believe he believes.

I was humbled that he even talked to me because he looked pretty tough.

I wasn't always sure what I was doing, but I prayed every day. I believe prayer does have an impact. I don't know for sure what or who God is, nor do I think I have the mental capacity to know. I think too often people try too hard to understand what or who God is, and that causes them to stumble, because there's no way we can absolutely know until we meet Him face to face. When I prayed through rehab and during my time in jail, there was change that happened. I can't quantify it. I was grateful for what I had in my life. My new friend seemed to understand this, and it clicked for him. Maybe he was a tough guy hiding behind his wild hair and body tattoos. Maybe he didn't want anyone to know his belief system.

You see, in jail, it doesn't matter who you were or where you came from. There was a commonality in jail, whereas there might not have been if we had simply met on the street. I accepted and surrendered to my situation and where I was. I belonged to this commonality because I had broken the law.

Journal Entries:

8/22 – Corrections officer showed up at work (driving range). Didn't recognize her and asked how I knew her. She said quietly, "In jail."

I apologized and said, "Well, I'm here." She said, "Just where you should be."

I thanked her for being so nice in jail and told her how that really helped me. I think there was a blessing in that moment as she could have been a jerk, but she cared enough to be discreet and not draw attention to me and my situation. She cared enough to not make a big deal about it or embarrass me, and I'll always remember that.

9/26 – Talked to fellow inmate in pod about his heartbreak with a girl who caused him a lot of problems. Told him that it hurts so much because love is like an addiction; at least falling in love is. When it's over, we focus on all the "love highs" and not the bad parts. Just like we focus on the drug high and not the withdrawal. We get nuts because we can't get that "high" anymore and we think we need that person to get it. That's why we become obsessed with that person.

10/10 – Guys in pod are getting irritable and hostile. Two argued and quit playing cards all about whether one washed his hands or not. Another guy was mad at me for a day because he thought I took too many cookies.

10/13 – In Bible study today, we talked about hell being completely dark and quiet. We are only left with our thoughts about what we did or didn't do with our life haunting us for eternity. That would surely be hell; much worse than fire. The fear of hell shouldn't make us be good, we should just be good to each other anyway.

10/13 – New guy in pod "Tommy" climbs up the bars in the pod like a monkey. He talks back to the guards and gets thrown in the hole regularly for disobeying them. He was wearing a blanket because it's cold in here. When they took a head count, he wouldn't take it off so he went into the hole again.

10/17 – Corrections officer asked what was happening and when I'd get back to Huber. When I told him I was hoping for 10/30, he said, "I hope so."

The other guard said he'd pray for me.

10/30 – Got sentenced today, Huber with probation. The corrections officers were very happy for me - I wasn't going to prison.

Reflecting on this entry, I had four trials in roughly a two-year period. For the last trial, I was still in Huber. The guards trusted me so they let me change clothes and walk over to court. When I was on my way to be sentenced on my last DUI, I walked into the courtroom and up to the bailiff and said, "I'm here to check in for court."

He said, "Whose attorney are you?"

I said, "No, I'm not the attorney, I'm the bad guy."

He replied, "I've seen you here before; you're not the bad guy. You're a good man who made some mistakes."

I cannot tell you how much that meant to me. It was very significant.

As I walked into the courtroom of the Washington County Courthouse, I noticed something I hadn't seen in my previous visits, framed paintings and photographs on the wall of former (retired and deceased) judges who served on the bench in Washington County. One of them was my godfather, who had died when I was a teenager in a car accident while driving drunk.

I remember standing in front of the judge, and he said, “I’m really on the fence about you. I want to put you in prison for three years.”

I had no emotion when he said this; I was so worn down at this point. There were a lot of reasons I did what I did, but there were no excuses. At this point, I was already in Huber for my last DUI, and the judge was either going to sentence me to added time in Huber, or send me to prison for three years. The judge ruled more time in Huber, a year and a half, and no prison time. I think I was relieved…

I was in an orange jumpsuit and shackles…humiliating. We had to walk back from the courtroom and down the hall back into Huber, my jail, which was connected to the courthouse. It was at this point that I was grateful I didn’t have to be transported to prison.

The sheriff’s deputy who was taking me back to Huber looked at me and said, “This is going to break the rules, but you’re not wearing those chains. There’s no way you should be wearing that stuff.”

That meant so much to me. The deputy knew I wasn’t a threat to society. It was a surprise, but it was such a blessing. If I had to walk back with the chains on, I figured *I did the crime, I’ll do the time*. But that Sheriff’s deputy, this kind human being, didn’t think I deserved that kind of severity for my crime. Another angel in the midst? I think so.

Journal Entries:

10/30 – The most beautiful things in life cannot be seen or touched, they must be felt with the heart.

10/30 – What has happened to us in the past which was painful has a great deal to do with what we are today.

5/12 – "Josh" wanted his bunk back. Josh got moved when I moved into the cell. When the cell emptied, he wanted his bunk back from me. I said fine and he didn't say thanks for anything. When I told him, you're welcome, he had no idea that he could have just said, "Thanks."

7/11 – I met Andy while waiting in the Huber area to get back into jail after work. We talked about why we were there and he told me that his life has never been better since his arrest. He has a new job, making more money and has been promoted. No matter how low you get, there's always hope.

7/27 –There was this young man, early thirties, a heroin addict. I met this man the first day I walked into Huber. These guys were playing cards, a game called Spades, and I said, "Hi, I'm Alex," like it was the first day of school or something.

"I'm Donny," another said, "Luke...Cool Hand." I was being made fun of. I didn't get it. I was so green. Later that night Donny came and talked to me about his struggle with family and heroin, and over the course of a year we talked a lot. He asked me, "Can I write a letter to the judge for you because you really helped me?"

So he wrote the letter to the judge and he gave it to me and signed it. In jail, sending out a letter is a big deal. Inmates can only send out two letters a week. Each inmate would get two stamped envelopes at the beginning of every week, and if you sent one out for someone else, it was a violation.

I informed my attorney of Donny's letter, and she said, "That's great. Send it to me."

The envelopes are given to the corrections officers unsealed so they can read the letters to make sure someone isn't sending out plans to escape or enable other mischief. But the officers aren't supposed to open or read any letters sent to an inmate's attorney. Apparently that rule was violated, because within a day or two the corrections officer came to our cell and said, "Hoffmann and Donny, I'm writing you up."

Now mind you, this was before my fourth conviction, anything on my record during my time served could have an effect on my upcoming sentence, and if it appeared I was a rule breaker or troublemaker, the judge could take that into account and extend my sentence in Huber, or worse, send me to prison and extend my sentence.

He continued, "You sent a letter out for Donny."

Donny gave me the letter my attorney wanted, and I sent it for him.

I answered, "Ok," because I wasn't getting anywhere with him, and followed up with, "I would like a meeting with the captain."

When I saw the captain, she said, "It's not a big deal if you get written up."

She literally said this knowing I could go to prison.

I looked at her and said, "If it's not a big deal, I would like in writing why you won't dismiss it."

She said, "Just send the letter."

I argued, "So are you telling me to lie and put

Donny's name on here and use his envelope? If I'm honest I'll be doing the same thing, but if I lie, then that's wrong too."

The captain looked at me and said, "Case dismissed."

That stuff happened all the time.

5/27 – My revelation: 'My purpose is Shay'...

I was going to focus on helping him.

5/28 – Other revelations of public services message on AA and not driving.

Week out of rehab, female attorney about 55 gets pulled over on her 4th DUI. She knows the law and that she is already arrested. Once done, as she sits in the car while the sheriff talks to her through the window she grabs down between the front seats, pulls out a beer and starts drinking it.

He went away.

7/23 – 'Cool Hand' Luke wanted to "suitcase" some chew and it got stuck. He missed recreation. Sitting with Donny, I asked, "How do they get drugs and chew in here?" 'Cause I was wondering if the jailers sold it to them. He looked at me and said while smiling, "There's only one way to get stuff in here Alex."

Finally realizing what he meant I just said "Ohhhhh," and left it at that. It's called "suitcasing your stuff."

Mad Dog

I got "Mad Dog" to read, and I taught him some things about life, and right versus wrong. He said he liked the book I gave him, and he said he was grateful of the way I shared my thoughts on life and doing the right thing to a member of the Wisconsin Outlaws.

"Mad Dog" was a member of the Wisconsin Chapter of the Outlaws motorcycle gang. He and I got to talking, eventually opening up to each other about our lives. I was not the type of person to open up to others, and neither was he. The fact that he was willing to open up to me made me willing to do the same, and I realized that we *have* to talk about the hard stuff; don't hide that you have a family member who is an addict. Talking about your hard stuff will get you feedback and will help you form some sort of resolution much quicker than working on your own. Until you do, you won't understand the impact you have on others and how positive that can be; this really didn't become clear to me until I was in jail.

It was interesting to me to see the paradigm shift in this hard criminal, Mad Dog. As I got to know him, I began to see him show remorse for his actions, showing emotion.

Spent the day with "Mad Dog." He belongs to Outlaws MC gang. We talked about the Outlaws gang, and how it worked and why. He told me a story about his girlfriend being rebuked at a church because of her clothes. So, he and seven Outlaws turned up at the church. The preacher thanked them for coming and kicked out parishioners who were treating her poorly.

He told me I do more in our pod for people than is done in his church.

I loved to read; I read a lot during my time in jail. Mad Dog told me that he had never read a book cover to cover in his life. I gave him a James Patterson book I really liked and thought he would enjoy as well. I encouraged him to read it, and he did.

The biker guy with eyes in the back of his head was reading the book, Three Blind Mice, by James Patterson I gave him a week ago. He said he liked it and said, "Ya know what? It's the first book I ever read cover to cover."

This gang member did something nice for someone and they pointed it out. Mad Dog said "I guess Alex is starting to rub off on me."

When Mad Dog and I were both out of jail and on probation, he asked if I would become a Universal Life minister, which can be done on the internet, and if I would officiate the wedding ceremony for him and his girlfriend. So, I got the ordination, and he picked me up to go to a friend's house to do the wedding. I remember him saying, "Hey, we're both convicted felons. We aren't supposed to be spending any time together!"

That hadn't occurred to me, but as soon as he said it, I started sweating bullets! The ceremony went off with no problem, and it was very nice. They were very happy with what I did. Mad Dog and his friends were very respectful; they showed me more respect than I think I deserved.

Journal Entries:

- An inmate was telling the story of driving inmates to a party on Water Street, using the prison van after work pick up...

If you have good behavior and a license, you may be allowed to drive the jail bus to pick up other "jailers" (inmates) from work. Also drop them off. Several times Donny would drive them downtown Milwaukee to hit bars on Water Street. His girlfriend would meet them all with fried chicken. They had a strict schedule and could only party for 30 minutes.

- Ruppert, an older guy, had gotten his DUI at a country festival. He was drunk riding a four-wheeler on a grass

parking lot. He got pulled over by a golf cart with police lights on it.

- On work release you can go see your doctor. You pay of course. I had a rash and the doctor said it was bug bites. He wrote a prescription telling the jail they had to remove all the bedding, mattress and give me a new one. The jail complained, "This doctor doesn't know what he's talking about." I replied, "I don't know, I don't have a medical degree." They made me remove everything and clean it up. The rash went away.

- One guy committed a crime "good enough" for prison so he could have the surgery he needed.

- Another guy was waiting in Huber to go to prison. Even to us it didn't make sense to be on work release when you were going to prison. He got out for work and hasn't been back since.

- I haven't had a drop to drink in 3 years. I made it through my son's death without even thinking about it. Most doctors call my alcoholism situational, and I survived many bad situations without a consideration of drinking.

- Guy in Huber nicknamed Santa; yes, he looked exactly like him. People would be talking at the dining tables, and he would be about five to ten feet away in his bunk.

Out of the blue he brought up, "Ya, I left my sweatshirt at work today."

No one was talking to him. He would sit on the phone talking to his girlfriend with baby talk. Now remember we're talking a very big guy with white hair and beard talking baby talk to his girlfriend while in jail. Meanwhile, Sinatra is singing on the TV, "Fly Me to the Moon." While on the phone someone farts in the shower.

Santa says, "Bless you" and goes on with his baby talk.

Then he says, "Honey, I'd marry you if you got divorced."

- Young kid comes into jail. He's really petrified. The other inmates pretend to be talking about going down to the pool to swim later that day. You guessed it, there is no pool. Eventually the kid works up the courage, "How can I get to use the pool? Can I go with you?" Very seriously the inmates say, "Sure, but you have to get a pool pass from the corrections officer." The kid prepares to ask the jailer, and the fun begins.

- There may be no pool but there is a basketball court on the roof. We can no longer use it because friends of inmates were tossing tennis balls up there with drugs in them.

- Inmates play Monopoly. Yes, at the beginning you have all these tough guys setting up and starting Monopoly just as if they are with their families. Eventually it leads to rule breaking, extortion of the other players, gambling, etc. A loser eventually knocks the whole board over.

- Wisdom from jail...Inmate making collect calls to radio station just so he has someone to talk to. They accept his calls...for a while.

- Trying to get my driver's license back I called the Alcohol Council as instructed. They said if you don't start the program by "x date you will be out of compliance." I said, "I have no money." They responded, "Then you're out of compliance." They said, "You will have twenty-four hours or you will be out of compliance."

I said, "Well I can't do anything on the weekend no one's open." They said, "You'll be out of compliance then."

- So the banker (that was me) works on a business plan for his boss while in Huber at night. Once finished he wants to take it to this boss when he's going to work. A "by the book" CO (Corrections Officer) stops him. CO Clark.

He says, "You can't take that paper out of here until you're released."

I ask, "Why is that, Officer Clark?"

"Because it could be plans for a jailbreak," he says.

"But Officer Clark, if I wanted to break out I'd just leave when I go to work and not come back," I say.

"Well you might be trying to break someone else out," he continues.

"But I can mail it out to someone or myself at work?" I rebuke.

"Well of course you can mail it out, you get two stamps a week!" he says. (Wisdom from jail…)

- Every so often a fire alarm goes off. Strobe lights going, quite the effect. Our jail door opens; no one comes, and no one explains what happens. Even inmates worry sometimes.

*- Huber inmates pay a fee to live at the jail when they get their paycheck. The employer is supposed to mail the check to the jail so we don't spend it and not pay the jail. Doesn't sound like a good idea since they already have you in custody, but who knows? The angry cook won't mail the check to the jail. His response is "F**k them; here's your check." The banker dutifully takes the check to the jail. The accountant says, "You're breaking the rules by giving me the check; you might get locked up and not be able to work."*

The banker says, "I understand, but you do want the

check, don't you?"

The accountant says, "Yes, but we can't tell anyone."

The banker says, "Tell anyone what?"

The accountant for the jail smiles, knowingly. Wisdom from jail...

- It was Bob's last day in Huber. He was to be released in an hour. He thought it would be funny to put shaving cream in his buddy's bed under the covers. After all, they were always playing gags on each other. The other buddy caught him. They exchanged words and ended up wrestling each other on the floor of the pod. He got another two days, and he had less than an hour until his release. I guess good humor has a price.

- Mike, a very fit young heroin addict who wants no friends in jail ends up training other inmates to get ripped in the recreation room. There have to be windows in any common areas so guards can see you wherever you are. One inmate went to the law library on certain days, at certain times so he could view the women exercising. He was quite the bookworm but he didn't get an appeal filed.

- Wisdom from jail...? Nate decides he wants two lunches and he's alone in the pod on a work day. He puts the shower on and when the guards come with lunch he says, "We need one more for Dave he's in the shower." They go fetch him another lunch. However, when the guard does the hourly walk through they quickly realize he's the only one there that day. He spends the next day in solitary. What could he have been thinking?

More wisdom from jail...

- Inmate came back from work and the accountant told him that he is behind on his weekly Huber fees by $40.00. Inmate told the accountant he's behind because

he worked outside, and it rained two days last week. Accountant jailer said, "Well you can't get out to work unless you pay the $40. You can't pay until Monday because it's the end of the day on Friday so you'll have to pay the additional days you're held in from work this weekend." Wow.

- Overheard: "Its Obama's year. Obama won because a black girl won on 'American Idol.'"

- Sage alcoholic states that "DUI's weren't a problem in my day. We had a hood ornament on our cars to line the car up with the road."

- Another inmate used dog pee to pass a urine drug test.

- In rehab, a patient said he was so depressed he tied a rope around his neck and jumped off a chair. When he jumped the cord pulled the curtains open and he realized it's a nice day out.

- When asked why letting water run for an hour in the sink Dusty said, "I'm not wasting it; I'm keeping my milk cold and I don't want to drink it quite yet. Anyhow, we pay for Huber so that includes the water."

- "Nathan" asked me how my day was tonight. I said, "Okay, not perfect."

He replied, "Don't wait too long for a perfect day."

There's wisdom in jail.

***

Looking back at my time in Huber was eye-opening; it broke open my soul and remolded my purpose in life. It was there I had my awakening. It had such an impact on me; it was just such a weird experience. It is amazing what we have to do to get through an experience like jail. You never know what you are capable of until you have to do it. I still ask myself how I got through all of it. It is hard to explain the depths of loneliness I experienced, even before I went to jail. I was ripped from a family I was extremely close to and had constant interaction with every day, and seemingly all of a sudden, it was gone.

During my time in jail and in the mission, I didn't know anyone or what to do. I was completely alone. Even when Shay was using, I experienced extreme loneliness because I didn't know what to do about it and that was tearing me apart. I don't have a good way to describe how paralyzing that kind of loneliness can be.

I think back to some of those darkest hours and wonder how I did it. I don't know how I didn't become more depressed to the point that I did something stupid. The quick answer is that I *had* to; I didn't have a choice, I just had to. I don't know how to explain it, but I got through it, because I had to, so I should be able to explain it, but I can't.

Maybe I had some sort of basic survival skills unwittingly kick in. The tough guy in me would like to say I had some sort of "street smarts." I have always been able to fit in wherever I was, and that may indicate that I have some sort of survival instincts. I try to create a rapport with people and try to understand their plight, as opposed to whining about mine, and that draws them in enough to have some sort of basis to at least deal with each other. Jail *is* the great equalizer.

I'll tell you without hesitation that there is no question that I had the help and support of some very good people and close friends. I still do to this day.

I had done well in each step of my career, and then suddenly I was in jail; that was tough to wrap my head around. I went from the top of my profession to nearly being beat up by a Latin King in jail. The journey was long and the struggle at times unbearable, but it led me on the course which shaped me into the man I am today.

The other inmates would often say to me that I got screwed by the judge for the sentence he gave me. But they are wrong. I wasn't screwed, I brought it on myself and needed to pay my debt to society for breaking the law. I was where I was supposed to be. To say a judge was wrong for putting me in jail is ludicrous.

The bailiff at one of my sentencings said that bad things happen, but that didn't make me a bad person. That was hard for me to accept for a long time. I am finally starting to buy into that concept.

What I have found—and this is worth repeating—is whether you have failed or faltered economically or whatever, you do what you can do about that problem. Once I've done what I can do about the problem, I let it go. It is as simple as that for me.

Attitude is everything. There is nothing to gain from being a jerk, negative, or getting angry and out of control emotionally, or throwing a tantrum. There is no scenario where you will get what you need from someone else if you treat him/her like crap, scream at them, and become unhinged or irrational. In fact, you will most likely get shut down, thrown out, arrested, or even physically hurt…but you definitely won't succeed.

My good attitude made it possible for the correctional officers at Washington County Jail to take compassion on me and let me see Shay at the hospital those days when he was in a coma after his overdose. That is very unusual, for an inmate to be allowed to do that, but they told me, "Just let us know where you are and what is happening," and they let me go to be with my son.

There were times when I was at Huber, when I came back from work, I would have to sit in the holding cell, for hours sometimes, waiting to be checked back in. That happened to everyone. A lot of the inmates would get really bent out of shape and start yelling at the Corrections Officers, saying really insulting things. That certainly didn't make the COs move any faster to get the inmates checked in. I have no proof, but I'm guessing they took their time. I would bring a book with me, then just sit in the holding cell and read until the officer got around to checking me in. I really believed they appreciated me not giving them grief about making me wait, and that contributed to their flexibilty with me when I went to sit with Shay at the hospital.

It was my attitude, always trying to stay positive, which also made it possible for me to get my driver's license renewed when I came off of probation.

My probation officer told me that I should write to the judge, and inform him of what I was accomplishing, and ask the people I worked for to write letters of recommendation to that judge as well, to see if he could get me my driver's license back. I had to take the letters to the Washington County Judge. The Washington County Clerk told me that, since I lived in Waukesha County, I had to appeal to the Waukesha County Judge. Keep in mind, I didn't have a driver's license, so I needed to get a ride to these courthouses. When I got to Waukesha County, the clerk told me that we needed to go and talk to the judge in Washington County. So back to Washington County we went. We saw the clerk there a second time and told her that we went to Waukesha County like she told us to, and they told us that Washington County was supposed to take care of it. The clerk was really annoyed with me and treated me like I was the dregs of society. She was not happy with me, and absolutely did not want to (nor did she have to) help me figure out what I was supposed to do. My friend who drove me was livid, and asked me how I was able to be so nice and polite and not go off on the clerk.

I said, "What's the upside to that? Sure, I can scream at her; I certainly have the capacity to, but what will I gain from that?"

I told the clerk, "You are correct, I don't live in Washington County, and I believe you, that you are correct that I have to do this in Waukesha County. I assume that you are right, but can you please just call over to the Waukesha County clerks and tell them they are the ones who I need to work with on this?"

She said, "I shouldn't do this but I will call them, and I'll print out the state regulations that say they are the ones to deal with this, so you can show them and they won't send you back here."

She was correct, and she helped me get to the correct place to get to the proper judge in the right county. I really think—in fact, I'm positive—that she would not have helped me figure that out if I had lost my temper and screamed at her. I was polite, respectful, and talked to her in a rational way.

This process took several months, but I did get in front of the correct judge, and he spent about thirty minutes in open court reviewing the materials and information about my charitable work from the owners of Yo Cool (more on this later), stating they needed me to be able to drive to my place of employment.

After the judge was finished reviewing that material, he said to me, "Mr. Hoffmann, based on all of this, you will have your license back immediately."

I thanked him. He wished me luck, and that was it.

The point of this story is to say, that if I hadn't behaved like an adult, and had pitched a fit to that clerk, I probably would *still* be wondering where to go and how to get my license back.

I walked out of that courtroom a little bit better. I wasn't any richer, I was still living in a room at a friend's house, life wasn't great, but it *was* a little better.

If you are struggling and don't appreciate moments like that—which may seem somewhat incidental, but are definitely not—if you don't take the time to be grateful you'll drive yourself crazy. A saving grace that has gotten me through all of this is being grateful for things that go well.

You can either crawl into a hole,
or you can do something.
There is light at the end of the tunnel
as long as you
keep your eyes open.

CHAPTER SEVEN

MY PIVOTAL MOMENT: 2012

A pivotal moment can be defined in all the moments that lead up to it... Life's purpose.

I was in jail thinking...*I'm old, how am I ever going to recover? I don't even have a place to stay.* At times jail was appealing because I didn't have a place to live and no resources to find a home. So, I said to myself, *ok, I know what I can't do; what CAN I do?*

I wish I could describe in words the real and raw feeling of having absolutely "nothing." There are so many people who have lost everything in life, and it's not just addicts. If you've lost everything or you've lost a loved one, you have to move forward and make a conscious choice to do something. You must continue to do more and more and more. It was in that moment at Huber, I realized God was truly speaking to me but maybe I just wasn't paying attention.

I still remember pleading with God, "Can you give me a sign?" I needed to know God was real and that He was with me.

My emotions were raw and I was lost. I had feelings of despair, loneliness, hopelessness.

I had been praying and praying. I read *The Bible* three times.

My prayers were for strength, courage, hope and direction. Early on I asked for things but I realized God doesn't give us things. God gives us the ability to get what we want. I knew what I could do…even if it was little things like praying…tapping into God, or the collective consciousness, whatever you prefer.

Then I finally realized He *was* giving me signs. This was another changing point. Signs like the deputy taking off those shackles, the bailiff telling me I wasn't a bad guy, people who got me to and from work, the Corrections Officer who saw me while I was at work but didn't say anything to embarrass me and encouraged me. Kindness shown to me by so many people was a sign. Some families going through what mine experienced get to a point that they scatter, but mine didn't. My kids stayed around, my brothers and sisters didn't leave me. Friends I barely knew from my jobs, such as the owners of Crossroads Restaurant and Swing Time golf driving range, were extremely kind to me and didn't desert me…also signs. Angels in the midst.

Again, I kept telling myself I can always do *something*. What can I do? *Do something*. I chased the guards in jail, and I asked, "Can't I mop the hallways?"

"There's a union; you can't," the guard replied.

"Can't I do AA meetings?" I asked, but I was told no again.

I wasn't negotiating a million dollar deal any more, but there had to be something I could do, and each day I did a little more. That awakening was a pivotal turning point in my life. I learned you can always do something, and if you're doing something toward solving a problem, then you're at least moving forward. I took my cues from that initiative. Even as small as those initiatives might have been, it did something to my brain chemistry…to my soul, and something inside of me started changing.

Here's how I looked at it: I could decide what the problem was, decide what I could and couldn't do about it, and then just do what I could. It was a good strategy as long as I was doing something toward solving that problem. It made me feel better. And once I realized I'd done everything I could, I just had to let it go. I couldn't keep beating that problem to death. The most precious thing anyone has in this life is time. Why waste time on things you can't do anything about? I learned to do what I could and release it.

When I was out on work release, I was able to call Shay, Harley, and Nina more, asking about their lives. I wanted to focus on them rather than my circumstances. How were they doing in school and at work, with friendships; whatever they would share with me, I would listen. Not that I was shutting them off before, but when you're in jail, communication is a bit more problematic. I didn't have access to communication whenever I wanted it. But I focused on my relationships with them, building and moving forward. I asked them if they had any questions about the past but they wanted to focus on the future.

At one point, Shay and I were both in different jails; me

in Washington County, and Shay in Waukesha County as he had been driving home from class during his senior year at University Lake School and he was nodding out. He got picked up, and drug paraphernalia was found in his car.

While in jail, rehab, and counseling, he was seeing a psychiatrist. He continued to send me his words of encouragement and pictures he'd drawn.

I continued to think about all of my children the entire time I was in jail. When I was out on work release was the only time I was able to communicate with my kids. I still remember a specific time when I called Shay. I apologized for all the problems I had caused.

His reply still echoes in my mind, "Dad, you gave us a great childhood. You always did the very best you could for us. I'll always love you."

These words kept me going, kept moving me forward.

It was also during this time that I got the call from my oldest son, Harley, "Shay overdosed, and he's in a coma. It doesn't look good."

I was at work (out on work release) when I got that call. Memories of Shay flooded my mind, and those unconditional words he spoke to me one of the last times we talked, "Dad, you gave us a great childhood. You always did the very best you could for us. I'll always love you."

I repeated those words over and over in my head. It made the horror of what was to come seem less real. It made Shay seem more alive.

I was able to get a ride to the hospital from my friend

Jim Morrison to be at Shay's side. Shay never did come out of that coma, and we won't ever really know if Shay felt our presence in his hospital room during his last days. We don't know if he heard our cries, felt our hands holding his, or if he heard us tell him how much we loved him. I told Shay I'd never drink again, and I haven't. I won't. I never will again.

Shay died July 1, 2013.

My life would never be the same again.

Jim Morrison

Jim is a good friend. We met when I was working at the golf driving range. He is a golf pro and runs the pro shop at the range. Jim drove me to the hospital when I got the call that Shay had overdosed, and he also drove me there the day Shay died.

"Alex and I met at Swing Time. We struck up a friendship that continues today. The jail was on my route to the shop, so quite often I would pick him up and drive him to the restaurant for his second job and/or back to jail at the end of the day. I was happy to do it. It gave us time to talk. He was surrounded by negativity, but Alex had a positive attitude. I would always try to perk him up if he looked like he was getting down.

He went through some tough times, even before Shay passed. He went from the top to the bottom, but he handled it all well. Alex is an amazing individual with a drive to work on the problem of addiction and using his experiences with addiction and loss to help others. I really admire him for his efforts to help addicts and their families.

I drove Alex to the hospital the day Shay died. I'll never forget that day. I was so heartbroken and sad when I saw him walking out of the hospital; he walked out all alone with that piece of paper with his son's hand print on it. As we drove back to Washington County Jail, I just listened and let him talk about Shay. We drove past places close to their old house on the east side of Milwaukee, and he would say, "We played golf at that course over there," or, "That's where Shay went to school."

I think about that day a lot, and every time I do, it makes me cry. All of the battles he has been through, he has come out on top. We still talk all the time, and I'm inspired by his positive attitude, his work with Yo Cool, and his ability to rise above the bad things that have happened to him."

- Jim Morrison

We decided not to have a funeral for Shay. We celebrated Shay's life on two separate occasions, both a year after he died. We had a memorial Mass at St. Robert's in Milwaukee. A few weeks later, we had a memorial service at the Pfister Hotel in downtown Milwaukee. There were a lot of good friends, a lot of memories and pictures. My kids and their mom did a great job putting it together. It was hard to look at those pictures…

Both events were very heartfelt; Shay's friends were there, and he was remembered fondly and was greatly missed.

That same year, I was blessed with a gift...I did an hour tribute to Shay and my other children, Harley and Nina, on WKLH, a radio station in Milwaukee. I had never done anything like that before. The headphones were on, the microphone was in front of me, and God just gave me the words: "Good evening Wisconsin and the world. I am Alex Hoffmann and this is 'Hey Shay, we're on KLH!'"

I also remember sharing with the listeners, "We lost our son Shay on July 1, 2013. He was only twenty-two years old. This show is dedicated to our son and our children's brother, Shay Hoffmann. So here we go! Let's light this candle and everybody buckle up! A special shout out to my children Nina and Harley Hoffmann, and their mother, Randy. You have been through more than anyone should have to endure and for that I am very, very sorry. I will always love you."

As the show went on I thanked everyone for listening. I was so grateful for the time WKLH gave me. In my closing remarks, I offered this, "Please indulge me this additional thought. We are never promised tomorrow. Hug your children, your family, until they ask you to stop…then hug them again."

Afterward, a good friend asked me how I thought I did. I told him I had no idea but that it really didn't matter because minutes after the program, I received a text from my daughter. She said, "That was great, Dad!"

Those were the only words I needed to hear from the one person along with Harley who mattered most to me. My eyes swelled up with tears. *After that nothing else matters. That was all that mattered to me.*

Not only do I miss Shay very much, I miss all of my children. It's not that I don't hear from my kids, and I do see them as much as I can, but it's that this experience with Shay's addiction and death changed us all so much. We will never be the same.

Many friends lit up Shay's Facebook page after his death. So many beautiful words were written and photos were shared. It was my daughter though, whose words were so profound and touched me the most.

She said, "I had a dream about you last night, Shay. We were three again."

She was referring to Shay, Harley, and herself.

It broke my heart.

I talked with Nina and Harley about their memories of Shay as I was putting this book together. They truly love and miss their brother.

Said Nina, "I think there are too many stories to tell. I think the biggest thing I would want to say about Shay is that he was fearless and that is something I always envied or rather admired about him. Granted, his fearlessness got him into trouble from time to time, but he lived more than a lot of us in only twenty-two years!"

Harley remembered Shay, "He loved art; he was mainly a painter. There are so many things from playing soccer and model car racing, snowboarding at Snowstar every weekend, he and I learning to do that together, to skateboarding in the front yard for hours and hours."

"He liked to read and listen to music. He loved Bob Marley and other Reggae, classic rock like Zeppelin, Hendrix, and Boston."

"One funny thing I remember about him was that he made weird faces…all the time."

"You can't go back and
change the beginning,
but you can start where you are
and change the ending."

- C.S. Lewis

CHAPTER EIGHT

GET BITTER OR GET BETTER: MY PURPOSE

A man's self-worth can too often be found in his job…
A new hope!

After Shay died, I realized my life, as I knew it, was over. My son was dead. But I also knew, in my gut, that this problem—this opioid epidemic—was going to get worse. This wasn't just my son, this was hundreds and thousands of sons and daughters. I know I am not alone, and this opioid crisis *has* gotten worse over the years, and it is only going to continue to get worse. So I decided that as long as I woke up every morning, I knew I had another day to help others. I have committed myself to trying to keep people and families from going through what I did… losing a child to addiction…and do it in the name of my son, Shay Hoffmann.

I knew when my release day came and I reentered the world, I could continue to do something productive with my life no matter what path I chose.

One day, one of my prayers was answered.

My sentence in Huber was for about eighteen months, and with eight months to go, I received a call from Paul

Armitage, a local business owner. I had met Paul and his wife while I was on work release working at the golf range and Crossroads Restaurant, and we became friends. He told me about a new business endeavor he was putting together, Yo Cool Frozen Yogurt. He explained the theory and model behind Yo Cool, and he offered me the opportunity to manage this new business, from the ground up. I accepted this gift. It was a true blessing and one that I will always be so grateful for. I had nothing, and now I had something. Something that was going to help people, make a difference, and change lives.

Another friend whom I had met while I was working at the driving range offered to let me stay with him after my Huber release. I now also had a place to live; yet another angel in the midst.

I spent my work release working on the physical build-out of the new Yo Cool store in Menomonee Falls, Wisconsin. Close to the end of the build, I was released from jail, and on October 5, 2013, we had the big grand opening. I began my new job as the manager of Yo Cool Frozen Yogurt.

Yo Cool Frozen Yogurt is so much more than colorful toppings and a tasty frozen treat. It's a phenomenon that stands entirely on its own. I can still vividly remember the day my friend and owner, Paul Armitage, said to me, "All I want is for Yo Cool to cover its expenses. I'll be happy with that."

Giving away all of the profits? What businessman does something like that? The answer is a man who truly cares about people and giving back to his community, and that's the owner of Yo Cool, Paul Armitage. Paul is the owner of Service Heat Treating in Milwaukee, and he has given of himself entirely to help the community financially. No person could give more than he continues to give to help his community and state.

Yo Cool is not about drug and alcohol addiction; it's about helping individuals, families, and children in the community by having a positive influence in every way possible. It is a vehicle to help people in need, and a safe place for kids to hang out.

We feel one way to curb addiction is by building strong families. Families don't take the time to have dinner together anymore. They are fractionalized, and that is one of the factors that leads to addiction. Parents may not be able to get their kids in the same room for an hour for dinner, but they can certainly get them to sit down for a frozen yogurt treat and talk.

Since opening in 2013, Yo Cool has donated proceeds to hundreds of charities and helped thousands of people in need, while providing a safe and positive environment for kids and families. It's a great place to "chill" after a sporting event, school, or a meeting. It has filled a great need in our community. Yo Cool has helped me to understand the true meaning of giving, *really giving*, both personally and financially.

It's amazing to read responses about our mission from the public. Talking with customers at the store about their gratefulness is inspiring. Together, we share successes, failures, happy events and sad events. We talk about our children and our hopes and dreams for them. We laugh.

We cry. We are a unique community of separate souls.

Fourteen to sixteen hours a day, seven days a week, I am at the store. I'm usually tired and beyond exhausted, but that all fades away when I see the smile in the children's eyes and the true miracle they all are. Yo Cool Frozen Yogurt has brought me so much healing, joy and a newly integrated sense of "family."

Someone said to me,
"I don't know how you do it."
I said,
"I wasn't given a choice."

CHAPTER NINE

HELPING OTHERS: PERSONAL STORIES

There is hope in helping yourself...

It's helping others first.

I did make a promise to Shay that I would not have another drink. To this day I have kept my word, and I would rather die than break that promise. I hadn't been drinking for a couple of years at that point, and I wonder sometimes why I didn't start back up when Shay died.

The promise notwithstanding, drinking won't do me any good.

For a few years after my release from Huber, I attended weekly counseling sessions, Al Anon meetings and Alcoholics Anonymous/NA meetings two to three times a week. These meetings have helped me to better understand addiction and how the problem of mental illness and the current legal system exacerbates the condition.

The good news for me is that God has relieved me of that burden right now, but I am smart enough to know that I fear it entirely. I'm an alcoholic, and I can go back to it at any time.

One thing I learned in counseling is there are varying degrees of alcoholics. Some guys would say, “I just think about drinking every minute of every day.” I believe them, but I wasn’t thinking like that. I’m not completely sure why, but I do know one difference is that I am more productive and have more energy because I’m not drinking, and I try to focus my energies on doing other things. If you can get a focus, somewhere else to direct your energies, the idea of drinking lessens. Maybe not as mine has, but it does diminish. I think a lot of alcoholics and drug addicts are bored and don’t know what to do. But there is always something to do, like work at the Salvation Army where you can help and interact with people who need help.

It was like when I started working at Yo Cool. I began meeting people and that began opening me up to other things, meeting other people, getting noticed by media and doing interviews for the newspaper and local television about the charitable work that Yo Cool does, using that attention to make contacts with folks in government positions who share the understanding of the immense scope and danger of the opioid crisis. Little things started opening up and I wasn’t bored; I was able to concentrate my energies on *doing something*.

***

I can’t really explain it. It may be a coincidence, but I still get goose bumps when I talk about it. In the last couple of years I met a woman who asked me to help her with her son. He was using heroin and had a mental disorder not unlike Shay. She knew we lost our son and did not want to lose hers. I found a treatment center that worked with dual-diagnosis patients, and she was going to tour the facility to see about having him admitted. Not too long after that, I received a message from her husband stating their son had overdosed and died. I texted a few friends to pray for him and the family. One friend texted back that he would gladly pray for them and asked what the son's name was. I never knew his name. I didn't want to bother the family at their time of grief, and I didn't want to lie either. I remember looking up and saying just that to God. I said, *You know who we are praying for so I am going to pick a name at random and pray for him*. I texted my friend a name that I felt God spoke to me...Dan. Several weeks later I saw someone who knew the family. I asked how they were doing and got information on the funeral. At the end of our conversation, I asked, "By the way, what was their son's name?"

She responded, "His name was Dan."

Special thanks to my angel again.

A lot of people come to me and ask me what they can do after the loss of their child to addiction. Usually, it is after the child has died, but sometimes people will ask what they can do with their son or daughter who is an addict. My answer depends on the addict and how he or she is reacting to the offer of help.

I do have a lot of mothers coming to me for help with their child who is an addict. I talk with them and give them the benefit of my experience; tell them that they aren't crazy and there really aren't any good answers, and, "You aren't out of your mind...you're just missing it. You must face the reality and don't deny it once you know about it."

Interestingly enough, fathers seem to back off, or

go quiet. Many are angry with the child and don't want anything to do with the situation.

The mothers will say something to the effect of, "My husband doesn't really get involved," or, "He was so angry and now he doesn't even talk with the child."

People always say to me, "I want to do something"... well, there's a lot you can do. We can *all* do *something.* The question is, *is it enough?* My theory—I suppose drawing from my business experience—is to take a top-down approach to getting people involved. There are people at the "bottom," doing the work and being directed and tasked with the "what" to do; but there are also committees to serve on, charitable organizations to give to and work with, etc.

I had a mother ask me what she could do about her daughter. The first question I asked her was if her daughter was willing to get help.

She said, "She is, but when we set it all up, she doesn't do it. She ebbs and flows with her commitment to recovery."

My response was, "If you don't do this, she's going to be dead."

I felt like a jerk for saying it like that. But it got through to her. She really dug in her heels and took the recovery process with her daughter to another level...a successful level...The hard love kind of level.

"What are you doing for her? How can you box her into the commitment? You tie it together; repeat what she says: 'You want help?' and she says, 'Yes,' even though she's probably just saying it to buy more time to continue to get more drugs and feed her addiction, and to get you to let up on her. You now have her committed to that; now YOU have to stick to that."

Because what addicts will do, and what I was trying to get through to her, is try to make you feel as good as they can for the moment, and then they'll go do what they were going to/need to do anyway; they just give you a glimmer of hope that they really are going to get help and turn their addiction into recovery. What many parents and loved ones who are new to this experience don't realize is that they are getting their chain pulled. They have that glimmer of hope for that day, those hours, that things are moving in the right direction, and that makes them feel good. So sometimes the only way to get through to the families is to deliver a punch of reality to the gut: If your child doesn't get to a rehabilitation facility and really commit to recovery, they will die.

There are really only three places an addict can go: rehab, prison, or the grave.

Well, she did stick to it, and I told her the next step was to get her detoxed, and for her (the mother) to go with the daughter to talk to some different rehab centers to figure out which they were all the most comfortable with. It is all based on what she already told you; that she wants help. You have to keep pushing the commitment. And you have to move quickly because, one, she may be dead—any time she puts that needle in her arm could be the fatal shot—and, two, as long as you keep the time frame short, based on her commitment, you have a much better chance of making this happen and succeeding; and you as the parents need to stand firm on keeping that commitment. And they did.

That mom and I talk occasionally, and she reminds me of what I told her; that if they didn't do this and go through the tough stuff, her daughter would be dead, and that I've seen it too many times to be wrong about it. She tells me every time we talk that those words were the reason she pushed harder than she would have to get her daughter into rehab and on the way to recovery.

That girl is now about a year into recovery, which is great, but it's no guarantee that it is going to stick. It takes at least twelve months for the body to get back to feeling well and the mind to realize that life can be good. The dopamine and serotonin start regenerating, but it takes a long time. Three, or even six months into recovery, the body isn't getting the chemicals rebalanced enough, and will still feel pretty lousy, and the recovering addict will still want to use. It comes back to the commitment. The addict must say, "I'm in this full bore, and however painful this is going to be for a year, I'll deal with it."

But the body is fighting back, saying, "No. You need to feed me!"

The process *is* painful. It is difficult to stick with; to make the adjustment to a new way of living. I knew when I got out of jail, even though it wasn't a recovery issue, that the transition would be really painful for a couple of years. I had a felony, which means I can probably never go back into banking and finance. But, I put my head down and put one foot in front of the other, and life got better little by little.

Teen Challenge, a ministry/faith-based recovery

organization, requires its clients to stay for an entire year for that very reason. They actually allow recovering addicts to stay free of charge—*if* they stay the entire twelve months. If they leave early, they have to pay.

When an addict is in recovery, it is important for them to become involved in other things and in actually helping other people; that is a huge step to staying clean. They need to keep focused on passions. When Shay was in recovery, he focused on painting and drawing, and playing music. They must fill the gap, the hole that is in them. Whatever put that hole in them, the drugs are filling it, and they need to fill that gap with something else.

As I mentioned earlier, there are only three ways an addict will end up: in rehab, in prison, or dead. As long as death is on that list, you have to do everything you can to help the addict. You have to be a jerk and lay the hammer down, if that is what it takes—and that usually *is* what it takes. It sucks. It disrupts the entire family. You have a family one day, and the next day it's all over the place. It's like your're heading down the hill on a train and the wheels are just flying right off.

I feel I have to tell the people I talk with and counsel the harsh realities of the struggle they are looking at; but also tell them the fight is worth it when they get their child back from the hostage taker that is the addiction. Because I went through the tragedy of losing my son to addiction, if nothing else, I can use that experience to try to save another parent from losing a child. I can hopefully keep another parent from going through what I did.

I believe it would be a tragedy if I don't use my knowledge and experience to save someone's life.

There must be hope.

We can *all* do something. It doesn't matter what your station in life is.

"Substance abuse isn't random;
rather, it's the byproduct of
unhealed mental and emotional pain."

From Addiction and Mental Health Demystified
With Joe Koelzer and Colleagues

CHAPTER TEN
FIGHTING THE FIGHT

A man's passion is found in his need to make a difference, to change lives... Take action.

Addiction in the United States—every single state—is an epidemic. That really isn't a secret; you can hear that phrase when you turn on the news. Politicians from city and county leaders, to county and state governors and legislators, to the President of the United States, have said, in one form or another, that addiction, and specifically opioid addiction, and especially heroin, and lately, fentanyl, is an epidemic that is getting worse and needs to be fought at every level of government.

The issue of addiction and mental illness transcends politics and party lines, race, economic status, or any other factor. It is not a Democrat or Republican, rich or poor, male or female, black or white issue. This is a *people* issue, and people are dying every day from drug overdoses. It is an equal opportunity enemy, but we can all pledge to fight it. It is an issue that no rational person can be on the wrong side of.

People are becoming addicted to drugs every day, they are desperate to feed an addiction and are willing to do whatever is necessary to do it. They are not in control, they are slaves to a drug that is more powerful than they are, and they cannot find freedom without help. What is being done right now to fight the opioid crisis is not sufficient; there needs to be a new way, a new approach.

Drug-overdose deaths and opioid-involved deaths continue to increase in the United States. The majority of drug-overdose deaths (66%) involve an opioid. In 2016, the number of overdose deaths involving opioids (including prescription opioids and heroin) was five times higher than in 1999. Deaths from prescription opioids—drugs like oxycodone, hydrocodone, and methadone—have more than quadrupled since 1999. From 2000 to 2016, more than 600,000 people died from drug overdoses. In 2016 alone, over 15,000 people died from heroin overdoses. On average, 115 Americans die every day from an opioid overdose.[1]

According to the Wisconsin Department of Health Services, in 2016, 827 people died in Wisconsin from opioid abuse. From the year 2000 to 2015, the number of deaths due to opioids increased 600 percent from 81 to 568.

The number of drug-related deaths easily outpaces the number of homicides or traffic deaths in Milwaukee each year.[2]

BE AWARE

Fentanyl: the step up from heroin.

Pharmaceutical fentanyl is a synthetic opioid pain reliever that is approved for treating severe pain, typically advanced cancer pain. It is 50 to 100 times more potent than morphine. It is prescribed in the form of transdermal patches or lozenges and can be diverted for misuse and abuse. However, most recent cases of fentanyl-related harm, overdose, and death in the U.S. are linked to illegally made fentanyl. It is sold through illegal drug markets for its heroin-like effect. It is often mixed with heroin and/or cocaine as a combination product—with or without the user's knowledge—to increase its euphoric effects.

I was able to get a meeting with a member of Wisconsin Attorney General Brad Schimel's staff. He was impressed with my knowledge of the opioid crisis as well as my passion for solving the problem based on my personal experience and desire to help others not to have to go through what I did. On a strictly volunteer basis beyond any personal advancement or recognition, he asked me to help him tackle the opioid problem in Wisconsin.

When elected on November 4, 2015, the Attorney General pledged to put public safety over politics. He continues to fight the opioid crisis in the state of Wisconsin. I met with Attorney General Schimel to discuss the addiction problem in Wisconsin, and I continue to meet with him occasionally in Madison. My work with him led to the opportunity on August 7, 2014, to meet Wisconsin Governor Scott Walker. Governor Walker and I discussed with him the possible solutions to the problems facing our state and what our state government can do about it. We have met on several other occasions since then to continue that discussion.

On January 15, 2016, I pled my case to Governor Walker for developing a strategic plan to battle addiction in Wisconsin and our country. Our meeting resulted in my assignment to work on that plan.

I see the solutions to the addiction crisis needing to be addressed in four categories: **addiction**, **mental illness, law enforcement**, and **societal norms;** and I began by focusing on what I saw as the issues that were hindering progress in solving the opioid crisis. The largest road block (as it usually is) involves communication and coordination of information. The drug and alcohol epidemic is so difficult to solve because it involves so many different parts of our society.

Interwoven together are drugs, alcohol, families, counselors, doctors, lawyers, employers…the list goes on. There are many people involved, and many organizations trying to help, but it's very fractionalized. As far as I know, there is no national database of information to help people in trouble or to assist families in trouble. Are we refining the system to find out what's working, or what's not wrong, and sharing that information with all of these organizations?

I realized there are many "silos" in the state, including the Attorney General's office, the Department of Health Services, Law Enforcement in general, the Justice Department, Department of Corrections, a department that regulates prescriptions and prescription shopping, and others. All of these different entities were separate but sometimes overlapping with little coordination or communication, which I saw as an inefficient use of resources. The corrections system needs to use punishment tempered with rehabilitation for individuals based on their situation. Grade school, middle, and high school students don't have a safe venue to share any of their problems confidentially (not just with drugs and alcohol) and to get the help they need.

Understanding Underlying Causes of Addiction

There is much evidence that a gene in the body contributes to, and perhaps causes addiction. At the very least, it makes one more susceptible to the problem. Alcoholics Anonymous and Narcotics Anonymous, as well as major rehabilitation centers promote, and rightly so, the "I am an addict or alcoholic" mantra, and how to avoid getting into trouble. However, very few focus on the underlying problems that are causing the addiction to bloom. The unresolved issues, problems, and pain are contributing to igniting the addiction along with the use of substances to avoid dealing with these situations. Addicts need hope, discipline, structure, and guidance. More has to be done to help addicts and alcoholics deal with the underlying issues and causes, and to resolve them. If that is done, the addict can focus on his or her recovery and then move forward.

Mental Illness

Mental Illness is inextricably tied into this issue as well. Whether the illness is full blown or just under the surface, it permeates the problem on several levels. Within the family structure, friends, jails, probation…it appears over and over. People with mental illness are generally in pain. When the pain is intolerable, they self-medicate. Whole families will self-medicate in order to deal with the family member with the mental illness; and the problem grows exponentially. The legal system is very deficient in this area. They have no idea what to do with mentally troubled individuals, specifically those with addiction problems. Much more has to be done in this area.

If something is not done now, we won't recognize our state, or country, in five years. As one director of a major New York Rehabilitation Center said recently on national television, "If you're not aware of the drug problem now, you will be."

All law enforcement officers, probation officers, and jail corrections officers who aren't trained in mental health, need to be able to hand cases to a mental health professional, and need guidelines and identified best practices to deal with those incarcerated for non-violent drug offenses.

Law Enforcement and the Legal System: Addressing the Cost of Addiction Incarceration with a Better Mix of Rehabilitation and Punishment

In 1980, there were approximately 500,000 people incarcerated in the United States. In 2015, that number grew to 2.1 million people. Including on parole, probation, or locked up in either local jails or state or federal prisons, that total comes to over six million people.[3]

A large number of these people have committed nonviolent offenses. This dramatic change is due to laws and sentencing guidelines related to the "war on drugs."

Many crimes related to the sale of illegal drugs are nonviolent crimes. How do they compare to the sale of legal products that are unhealthy or dangerous like tobacco, alcohol, or guns? I have been told that eighty to ninety percent of the offenders in Washington County Jail are there for non-violent drug and alcohol offenses.

In the federal system alone (a fraction of the United States prison population), there are over 90,000 prisoners locked up for drug offenses, compared with about 9,000 for violent crimes.[4]

On the other hand, some people are way too comfortable in prison. They seem to have forgotten the world that exists on the outside. They try to adjust and acclimate, yet remain ready to go home every single day. It's not easy to do. The truth is, the prison and its residents fill their thoughts, and it's hard to remember what it's like to be free, even after a few short months. They spend a lot of time thinking about how awful jail/prison is rather the envisioning their future. Nothing about the daily working of the jail/prison system focuses its inhabitants' attention on what life back on the outside, as a free citizen, will be like. The life of the institution dominates everything. This is one of the awful truths of incarceration, the horror and the struggle and the interest of a prisoner's immediate life behind jail/prison walls drives the real world out of his/her head. That makes returning to the outside difficult for many prisoners.

We need to focus more on rehabilitation in tandem with punishment. Drugs and alcohol are symptoms of a problem. *The problem is addiction*. Take one substance out of the way and the addict will find another.

Why are we putting alcoholics and addicts in jails where they receive minimal rehabilitation or none at all? Why don't we put them in mandatory rehab and then halfway house centers instead? Considering the overall cost of housing prisoners and building more jails, I believe we would save, or at the very least, more efficiently use taxpayer money to provide a positive solution to this problem.

I believe we need to work on the rehabilitation piece as well as preventing the problem before it gets to that point. Tied into prevention and rehab is the legal system and what we're doing with people who have addiction problems. We are focused on punishment, which is fair, but we aren't focused on motivating the good behavior we want. We're turning out more intelligent and committed criminals instead of people who have hope and can be productive in society.

One such example is how we view alcohol and drug addiction. Clearly, I can understand charging someone with a felony at some point. However, once that's done why not give them incentives to have that felony removed, for example, if there were no violent behaviors after a certain period of good behavior? If we keep saddling alcoholics and addicts with felonies, they lose hope. What can be done to give them hope? We can give them goals and incentives to correct bad behavior. If they are indigent, low on the income scale, and are having a very difficult time pulling themselves up, the possibility is that they will go back and use again. The lack of hope or of a clear way to correct their problems is almost inviting them to continue some kind of criminal behavior. I know this to be true. I've seen and heard it all too many times.

There's disrespect for the legal system and the laws by all age groups. Not just the addict, but the families and friends surrounding the addicts. This is due in part to laws, rules, and decisions being made that at times are inconsistent and illogical. On its surface, this may appear petty, but I believe that erosion will cause a breakdown in our society, especially in the area of the rule of law.

Prisons may have better opportunities for rehab and education. I don't know; however, county jails, which are the first step towards prisons, are entirely inadequate to help the offending addict. Counseling programs, job skills training, life counseling are very inadequate. Inmates need advocates to help them work through life and business issues as well as shown how to work through the system. Several attorneys have told me they'd be willing to do this and that it's needed, extremely needed.

Once out of jail and on probation, inmates need direction from others than a probation officer. Inconsistencies develop at this level as well, and an oversight committee to monitor and make suggestions is needed. This would help to bring balance and increase faith in the system.

There is little hope when coming out of the system. Without hope, many inmates turn back to drugs and alcohol for comfort and support. There need to be incentives for good behavior and for improving their lives. Yes, improved life should just be the incentive, but it's not. There's a connection, and incentives like dropping felonies after a period of time for good behavior would help. They would begin to see that good behavior will improve their lives, and the lives of those around them, but it takes time, and they have to learn to be patient.

Scholarship programs, grants, and school loans should be more readily available for inmates and parolees with good recovery behavior as well.

Programs should be set up to encourage offenders to turn themselves in to get help and stop the cycle of addiction. Motivation provided by getting help and a lesser sentence is needed. If they know that they can work off the stigma of a felony over time with good behavior, they have a great incentive, a goal, and hope.

A lengthy term of community service working with addicts while in jail and on the outside might drive home the truth of how addicts' and dealers' behavior and choices are complicit in their suffering and the suffering of others.

There is confusion and wide inconsistency in the probation and parole system, particularly when it comes to parole and probation interaction with alcoholics and addicts. There needs to be more training for the officers and better referrals to professionals for help. There also needs to be some type of oversight outside of the system to give help, suggestions, and even criticism.

Safe Haven Programs: I believe that more Safe Haven Programs should be set up to encourage offenders to turn themselves in, or to encourage their friends and families to turn them in, in order to get help and stop the cycle of addiction. These programs could be incentivized by providing a lesser sentence, if needed, or by allowing them to work off the felony over time with good behavior and completion of the program.

Offer More Effective DUI Sentencing Alternatives: all DUI convictions result in the offender's driving privilege being taken away. The length varies based upon the nature of the offense, but there is no avoiding loss of one's license. The offender is not allowed to get an occupational license for at least a month, and maybe even years. If the person is in Huber, they have a very difficult time getting to work. This prompts many offenders to use that fact as an excuse for not working, or they drive illegally in contempt of the law and the legal system. They lose the possibility of getting back on their feet, or they learn to disregard the law. Furthermore, to find rides, they ask other inmates, who may be much more experienced criminals, for help. Now they are indebted to that criminal and they are associating with more and more criminals on the outside. We're leading them right down the wrong path.

We do have breathalyzers for automobiles. Why not let the offenders keep their licenses immediately but with mandatory breathalyzers? If they can't afford it, then work out something so they can. That way they can go to work, pay taxes, find hope, and begin to move forward as a productive member of society.

With driving comes responsibility. The offender begins to return to society, with structure, payments, insurance, and the ability to aquire work and accept responsibility.

Societal Norms

The addiction and mental health crises, I believe, need to be treated before, during, and after the addiction and mental health problems occur; the emphasis on the *before* is essential. Societal norms need to be addressed. Failure is part of succeeding, yet an entire generation of kids has not been taught that it is okay to fail; to come in second place, to lose a game, etc. Kids have not learned to fail. They get a trophy for every game whether they win or not, and they don't connect the idea that failure is not the end of the world. I worry that kids are going to believe that they are always supposed to be happy. And if they aren't, they have to take something to ensure that they stay happy. At some point in our societal evolution, someone decided that kids should never be sad, and if they aren't happy for whatever reason, they are drawn to take a pill in order to be happy all the time. It is important for them to know that they don't have to be happy all the time, and to work through the bad feelings instead of masking them.

In elementary school, kids need to be directed to a place they can talk about their feelings: the bad, the good, the weird. They also need to know that it is okay to fail, to learn from failure and keep moving forward, and that only getting positive feedback is not real and not healthy. I don't like being unhappy any more than anyone else, but it is a part of life.

Jail is a pretty miserable place. While I was in jail, I was very unhappy, and I was in unbearable pain when Shay died. When I learned to accept it, that was when I had let the pain overwhelm me, I took the time to accept it, accept what I could and couldn't do about it, and then I was able to move out of that place. It wasn't easy, of course, but it was the only way I could get through Shay's loss without turning back to substance abuse, or medicating myself to "deal with" that pain.

What I learned was that you are going to have periods in your life when you aren't happy, or in some cases, life really sucks. When I went through those periods, I eventually realized that there might not be anything I could do about it except do my best to get through it. If there wasn't anything I could do about it, it was certainly counterproductive to just obsess over it. I am not saying this is easy. Kids need to (and sometimes need help to) get past those sad periods instead of turning to alcohol or drugs, or even buying an expensive product for temporary relief, that brief moment of happiness. They need to lean into it and absorb it for a short length of time; it will get better. Instead, a common solution— what has become a societal norm—is to mask the sadness and bury it under temporary fixes.

It is societal norms like that which need to be addressed, and at the grade school age level, before the addiction cycle even has an opportunity to seed. Standardized, composite programs like "Health and Happines" classes are where kids are taught why they take care of their bodies, and what they put into their bodies and why, and that it is not a good idea to try to put something in your body to try to change your mood because it is a temporary fix. You won't have solved any problems. My fear now is kids who end up gravitating in that direction. There also doesn't seem to be any attention given to dishonesty being a short-term solution to avoiding conflict or keeping from getting in trouble. By that I mean, say you have a problem at your job and you decide to avoid it by lying to your boss and telling yourself, *If I tell this lie, my boss will be off my back for now*. The problem is the boss may or may not circle back to you about your lie, but you still have the same problem, you haven't solved anything, and you aren't happy anyway. And, whether the boss finds out about your lie or not, you're still worried about it the whole time.

There needs to be a way to show kids that there are resources available for them to be able to talk. The same is true for any age group, really. People need to know what resources exist and are available to them

Addicts need to talk about their reovery. They need to get their recovery story out to raise awareness, and personally, for encouragement to continue with the recovery process. It's like going on a diet and not telling anyone. That can be pretty ineffective. There is strength in numbers. Talking about their addiction and recovery will keep them focused on stopping or rehabilitating themselves. It will also allow people to hold them accountable, and they will be more successful because people who know can help, as opposed to keeping it a secret and white knuckling it on their own. People need to know that they shouldn't treat their addiction, and family members shouldn't treat the addict, as an embarrassment or this issue as a stigma. The success in recovery and living a clean life is to get the word out there and receive help and encouragement from others. I am the poster child for this. I am an open book about my problems, and I am successful in my recovery. Nobody likes talking about the bad things they have done, I certainly don't; it is difficult. But I believe keeping it to yourself allows the subconscious to fool you into thinking that it is not something bad, because nobody knows about it so they aren't reacting negatively. The subconscious is in conflict with the conscious and that will doom you to failure.

Dr. Scott Peck wrote a book a few years back that I highly recommend. It's called *People Who Lie*, and it addresses this very issue. I base some premises of this platform on his concepts. Peck believes that if you continue to lie to yourself and restructure the truth to make yourself not look that bad to your subconscious, the conflict between the conscious and subconscious can send you down the path of either mental problems or the sociopathic behavior of minimizing bad things and just doing more of them.

The 911 Response

I began to envision a coordination of information between all of the state government departments and physicians, mental health, and other medical professionals, addicts and their families, charities, churches, law enforcement agencies, schools, and the legal system. I think all the information should be computer-based so the various groups can not only learn at a faster rate what the others are doing, but also quickly take advantage of what works and learn from what doesn't. When federal funding is received, everyone should have visibility of how efficiently those resources are being used, compared to what has been done in the past. All these factors would need to be considered to streamline procedures and solutions to help addicts recover and rehabilitate, and even keep people from starting to abuse drugs. All of the information needs to be shared to leverage the people working in the individual departments to design a synergistic approach to a better use of resources and assets. This way, the departments will be more transparent and the Governor (the guy at the top) would be able to best determine the most appropriate distribution of resources and assets.

When I began writing my strategic plan, I was reminded of the attacks on our country on September 11, 2001. I have no doubt that part of the reason that attack happened was the lack of shared resources and intelligence between the NSA, CIA, and FBI.

I called my proposal the *911 Response to Addiction.*

Part of the plan is to incorporate artificial intelligence (AI) to use all the information to establish the questions that need to be asked to follow up on use of funding, and coordinate communication between all the aforementioned departments and groups. This goes back to kids needing a resource to discuss their anxiety or depression, and adults getting the help they need that they don't even know exists for mental health issues. The AI should also help in the expediting of decisions, and getting more efficient responses. At present, the process of making a decision to do something about anything is so inefficient, and responses in government are infuriatingly slow. Imbedding an efficient way to finalize decisions in the artificial intelligence will facilitate a more favorable outcome. While the politicians drag out their decision-making processes, more people are dying. We don't have time to delay.

Wisconsin Attorney General Brad Shimel has been meeting with people from IBM (and I have been an observer and contributor at those meetings) to develop that AI to help people find the resources that exist to help them, and they have been beta-testing this first tier of the program in Los Angeles and San Diego counties in California.

Collecting medical information is a key part to this coordination working effectively.

There are prescription drug monitoring programs that would allow medical providers to record level one prescriptions in a centralized database, where other doctors, pharmacists, law enforcement personnel, or medical examiners can check those prescriptions; and where doctors can find out if patients are using multiple doctors and have prescriptions they have not revealed. With this system, doctors can cross-check the database to ensure their patients are not doctor shopping or seeking level one medications they already have. Police can check the system as well in the course of investigations.[5]

If the addicts allow HIPAA to release their information, state resources can help them form a plan to get them in rehab and focus on their recovery or to lace them in an environment to keep them away from problem people and areas. Probation officers can have access to an addict's health information and get them access to social, medical, or consulting programs to assist them in getting the help that they may not even know exists.

This is a strategic plan that, among other things, appoints a non-politician in a non-paid position, as a sort of

"Heroin Czar," to oversee and use the artificial intelligence technology; to orchestrate communication and information sharing between law enforcement, medical professionals, non-profits, and families who are trying to do something; and follow up on plans already initiated to ensure they are effective and there are no unintended consequences; and to make sure that resources are being used effectively. The total focus of this position is combating and solving the addiction crisis in the State of Wisconsin. There are no other duties or distractions.

The directors, or stakeholders, at the "top" will share the information between one another to pass down to their various related sectors, to look at overlap between departments, and to be sure each department is directed toward it's highest and best use and effectiveness.

The person who holds this position really should have experience with addiction and its effects on the family. I believe I have the credentials and experience to hold this position. It may seem, to some, to be a bad idea to have a recovering alcoholic and felon run a state agency. But, I would argue that, someone like me, with my knowledge and reputation that I know as much or more about addiction than most politicians and government staffers, would be the perfect person to hold this job. I am the "poster child" that I mentioned earlier.

Other duties of the suggested position:

- Develop short, medium, and long-term plans (mentioned above) for the State, addressing addiction (before, during, and after), the legal system, mental illness, and societal norms.

- Take on the leadership role in leading the fight of the opioid crisis by implementing and continuing to improve the 911 Response plan, as well as other directions and solutions that develop as progress is made.
- Follow up on laws, legislation, agendas, etc., to be sure the State is getting the intended results and that the resources are being utilized effectively to accomplish the intentions, and to make suggestions to improve and change, if necessary.
- Before any funding is directed anywhere, review federal and state money to be certain the resources are being directed effectively before those funds are released.
- Be accountable to oversight and review in one- or two-year periods. If progress isn't being made, a replacement can be appointed.
- Provide all state agencies "real-time" information that can be acted on quickly.
- Cull data and best practices from other states and countries to provide Wisconsin public officials up-to-date information to work better toward a solution. (I also believe we need to look not only at what other professionals and communities are doing to solve the addiction problem, but look also at solutions found in other countries).
- Work with people who have been affected by addiction and take advantage of their needs and pent-up energy to do something about it. Provide leadership to them and other parts of the private sector to get involved and stay active. Attend meetings as a speaker or observer, either in place of or with government officials or with various groups battling the addiction problem, and

upstream the necessary information to the decision makers in the State and Federal governments.

- Compile all the information gathered from all departments and entities involved and review the data and statistics (that the government is using to make decisions), and provide concise reporting.
- Find additional cost-effective resources for the different sectors that are battling the addiction crisis, including the government sector. Give feedback about what is working and what is not, without fear of reprisal or backlash.

Since my son's death, I've submitted information relative to my 911 Response. There has been progress in implementing parts of the plan, and the State of Wisconsin has budgeted for the development of the artificial intelligence and for someone whose time is devoted entirely to changing the paradigm of the opioid crisis in Wisconsin. It is my hope that eventually all of my plan will be included.

A task force was started by Wisconsin Governor Scott Walker to work on the problem, and I have testified before it, telling my story and about Shay and his addiction, the mental illness caused by his drug use, and his overdose, and sharing my thoughts and ideas of how to solve the addiction crisis. The task force is co-chaired by the Lieutenant Governor Rebecca Kleefish, and State Representative John Nygren. I'm grateful that it was put together. I'm grateful there were many people on the task force who held the degrees and had the expertise required to talk about the problem. I'm grateful that I was able to testify before it, and that my testimony, and that of the testimonies of other people who testified the day of the hearing, were recorded to be heard by the people on the task force. But none of those people were actually *at* the hearing, except the Lieutenant Governor, and Representative Nygren. It bothers me that these kinds of things that keep this issue mired in committees and people just only *talking* about doing something. The logic, as it is a lot in politics, is more reactive than proactive. I could tolerate that if it were a water rights issue for a river or something, but I have a hard time with it when people are dying.

The task force called me to Madison...

I said to them, "I hear we're getting seven million dollars."

"Yeah, isn't that great!?" They were excited to tell me that they were really doing something.

"Okay, well, who is tracking that? Where is it *exactly* going? There may be a few ideas, but it is pretty obvious there isn't anyone with accountability of allocating those funds to specific actions that are working. Is there anyone tracking previous grants and funding to see what worked and what did not, to keep from wasting those resources?"

I look at this as a business, and I look at it as how can we best leverage the assets, because I always hear how these groups and agencies don't have enough money or funding.

I referenced my 911 Response and the position that I designed to do just those things, and I offered to do it—for no pay—but politics keeps getting in the way. There is overlap of departments and withholding of information. I was even warned that if I were to come to Madison to work on the committee that there were people who would be resistant to my presence because they would think I was there to take their jobs.

I get frustrated with politics, the government policies, procedures, overlapping of departments; all clearly a waste of funds. For example, I was talking with the chief of staff of an elected official, and we were talking about a lack of funds, but he wanted me to know that he did meet with a pharmaceutical company and they agreed to give us a discount on Narcan.

I said, “That’s great. Did you ask them to fund the projects that the government won’t fund?”

“Well, that’s a million dollars.”

I said, “I know. Did you ask them for a million dollars?”

“Well…no.”

I pressed, “Did you know that pharmaceutical companies right now have a reputation somewhere between a tobacco lobbyist and a used car salesman? You don’t think it’s possible that they would fork out a million dollars for some good press?”

***

I testified before the Wisconsin State Assembly Criminal Justice Committee for legislation in Wisconsin that was introduced by Representative John Nygren, who serves Wisconsin’s 89th Assembly District. Like me, he is personally deeply affected by the opioid crisis.

Representative Nygren’s bills I testified for:

1. Narcan: Allowing first responders to carry the drug Narcan, a drug that can reverse the effects of an opioid overdose, so it can be administered to overdose patients at the scene instead of waiting to get to the hospital.

2. Amnesty: Immunity from criminal prosecution for drug possession if they bring someone to an emergency room or if they call 911 because they believed the person was suffering from an overdose.

These bills and Representative Nygren's two other bills that he wrote, were passed and made into law. I am proud to have worked with Representative Nygren. He is a tremendous man and he has done so much work on this topic. He asked me for my input while he was writing his bills, and I happily talked with him about my experiences and thoughts. I give him a world of credit for fighting this fight, and I sincerely appreciate his efforts.

BE AWARE

Narcan: Stepping Up the Fight

Narcan is a brand name nasal spray form of naloxone, a drug that can reverse the effects of an opioid overdose. Some states now require its police officers to carry naloxone to revive people who have overdosed. Many firefighters, emergency medical personnel, and other first responders also carry naloxone. Naloxone comes in three forms, some of which are generic, and all are approved by the Food and Drug Administration for treating opioid overdose. Narcan and other forms of naloxone are available both by prescription and over the counter in some states. Many emergency room physicians will write prescriptions for patients they treat for opioid overdoses.

Family members of people who are addicted to opioids or heroin can also get Narcan without a prescription at pharmacies. CVS offers naloxone over the counter in 43 states, while Walgreens now stocks Narcan in all of its 8,000 stores nationwide. Walgreens also plans to educate patients about Narcan, including how to administer the drug. This effort, combined with the opportunity for patients and caregivers to obtain Narcan Nasal Spray without an individual prescription in 45 states, is critical in combating this crisis.[6] Narcan can cost around $130 to $140, for a kit that includes one or two doses. Depending on your insurance plan, you could have a copay anywhere from $0 to $20 to purchase the medication. Medicaid and Medicare cover brands like Narcan, but coverage varies by state. Some community-based organizations focused on treating drug addiction may provide Narcan for free.[7]

I have worked with State Representative Nygren and Wisconsin State Senator Alberta Darling, who represents Wisconsin's 8th Senate District, to pass other legislation that will save the lives of those troubled with addiction, and to develop programs to help those suffering from addiction in our jails and prisons. State Representative Nygren and State Senator Darling are committed to protecting, educating, and improving the lives of children. One of many things they worked on was the H.O.P.E. Agenda.

They announced this information in a press release on August 2, 2017:

> Statement from Authors of Recovery School on RFP Madison: On Wednesday, State Senator Alberta Darling (R-River Hills) and State Representative John Nygren (R-Marinette), the Co-Chairs of the budget-writing Joint Finance Committee, released the following statement regarding the University of Wisconsin's Office of Educational Opportunity issuing a request for proposal (RFP) for a Recovery School for students dealing with addiction issues.
>
> "This is a huge step in our fight against opioid addiction. Creating a recovery high school was a part of the special session on the H.O.P.E. Agenda to combat opioid abuse. We appreciate that UW's Office of Educational Opportunity acted so quickly to begin the process of authorizing a recovery school. Creating a safe and nurturing environment for young people to earn a diploma while they recover is a key component of the H.O.P.E. Agenda. Evidence shows that attending a recovery high school instead of going back to a residential high school immediately following treatment can set a student in recovery up for a substance-free future."

In 2017, Governor Walker worked on twenty-eight pieces of bipartisan bills targeting the opioid crisis in Wisconsin, and signed executive orders addressing what he calls one of the biggest challenges facing the state.

"We're not getting mental health treatment, particularly for our young people," said Walker. "Sometimes that self-medication becomes looking to opioids."

Wisconsin Attorney General Brad Schimel added, "These executive orders provide for grants for law enforcement agencies, and for prevention programs. They provide for moving forward on the hub-and-spoke treatment model."

One order would create the Governor's Commission on Substance Abuse Treatment Delivery. The commission would include the co-chairs of the Governor's Task Force on Opioid Abuse or their designees as well as representatives from the health care industry.

The other order would require the State Department of Health Services to create the Governor's Faith-Based Summit on Opioids for pastors and priests; develop best practices for police and emergency workers responding to overdoses, and develop statewide standards for data submission on people seeking addiction treatment.[8]

Executive Order 274, the “hub-and-spoke" treatment model, looks to designate regional hubs across the state that can act as resource distributors for facilities and addicts. The Department of Health Services will assign regional hubs in the coming months. Officials say, the sooner this happens, the better.

While enforcement and awareness are important, so is prevention. One of the ways anyone can help with that is by taking advantage of drug drop-off boxes. They are available at many police departments across the state.

The locations, as well as much more information,
are available at:
http://doseofrealitywi.gov/drug-takeback/find-a-take-back-location

There is concern that these measures, while positive on paper, are not going to do enough to help groups with boots on the ground. The task force is not going to report their findings for *months*. What's really going to happen today for the people who are going to overdose today, tomorrow, and the next day?

Grant money from the State Department of Health Services and the Substance Abuse and Mental Health Services Administration will go a long way toward combating the problem. It's not just the drugs. You take away the drugs and the alcohol and there's a person there who needs to be trained to have healthy behaviors and patterns. It takes months to actually get sober. The hope is to help improve an addict's environment. Many users find their immediate families suffer, and in the worst cases, their kids too. Programs would also help addicts heal. Services that are needed and provided with the grant money include: medicated assisted treatment, residential treatment, recovery housing, day treatment, individual and family counseling, and more.

Yes, grants will do a lot of good, but all the tools in the world can't solve a problem like addiction until the addict is serious about getting help, doing something different, and having that need and desire to change.[9]

***

It is important for me to mention that there is progress. Some of my suggestions have been implemented and worked on, and in general, there are things being done in the State of Wisconsin. I am very happy about that. Many people have been involved in this fight, and are working hard. I want to extend my apprecation to them for their participation.

When I first met with Attorney General Brad Schimel, I presented him with a draft of my 911 Response; a twenty-page document. He read every word of it, and when he and I met with the IBM people to talk about the artificial intelligence portion, when he had questions about it, he directed them to me, making sure what was being worked on was what I had in mind per my plan. He referrenced my paper several times during that meeting. He is serious about the opioid problem in our state, and I sincerely appreciate what he has done and what he is doing about it. I count him as a friend. He's a genuinely good person.

Representative Nygren has several leadership positions in the State Government, but he still takes the time to devote his attention to the opioid crisis. I am thankful to him for his efforts and for taking time to listen to me.

I am thankful, as well, to Governor Walker, Lt. Governor Kleefish, and all the people in the State Legislature and local governments, such as Waukesha County Executive Paul Farrow, as well as Wisconsin's United States Senators Tammy Baldwin and Ron Johnson, for taking time with me and for bringing and signing laws to combat these crises, and for not treating it as a partisan issue; for working together...This problem affects ALL of us, no matter how we vote, or where we are from.

Some other work I have been involved in:

- I have met with State Senator Darling, and with Ed Wall, and Tony Strevelor of the Department of Corrections to discuss ways to help improve programs on addiction in our prison system.
- I have met with Dean Stensberg, the Executive Assistant to Wisconsin Supreme Court Chief Justice Patience Roggensack, and with Dana Brueck, Wisconsin Department of Justice Communications Officer, to discuss other ways to work on the addiction and legal problems affecting our state.
- I have worked with Milwaukee's District 10 Alderman and Common Council President, Michael Murphy on Milwaukee's Heroin Summit. A City-County Heroin, Opioid, and Cocaine Task Force has been created by the Milwaukee Common Council. They have been assigned the responsibility to study the challenges of drug abuse in Milwaukee County, to address the issues and to find recommendations to present policy. "Our analysis of the data shows that drug overdose deaths continue to climb in our community," Alderman Murphy said. "While we have already developed a critical partnership to study this epidemic, the next step is to translate this data into action."

  As the primary sponsor of the legislation creating this task force, Alderman Murphy has announced it will be led by experts from the medical profession and institutions along with city government officials, community organizations, and the general public affected by this epidemic...people working together to find real answers to address these real issues faced by so many of our citizens. In partnership with the Medical College of Wisconsin, the data analysis by Alderman Murphy's office indicated the 2016 overdose figures are on record pace to bypass earlier numbers of heroin and opiate overdose deaths. Awareness needs to be heightened to prevent potential overdoses in the future. Milwaukee Aldermen Bohl and Murphy also helped. To find out more on how the Task Force and the Medical College of Wisconsin are building awareness and fighting off heroin and opioid addiction, please visit mkecope.com/

- I speak to people at different groups, recovery centers, and other organizations. I tell my story and share ideas about fighting the opioid crisis, both locally and nationally.
- I have spoken to and continue to speak to the residents at the Herrington Recovery Center in Oconomowoc, and Nova Counseling in Appleton, Wisconsin. They specialize in outpatient care for addiction and mental illness. This may be the first stop in an addict's challenging journey to recovery.
- I have been a featured speaker at the Milwaukee Heroin Summit.
- I continue to work with and refer clients to Carl Lockrem, Director of the Grand Avenue Club, which works with those afflicted with the challenges of mental illness and addiction. From their website:

The Mission of The Grand Avenue Club: To provide Milwaukee County adults who have experienced mental illness with an array of opportunities that will assist them to experience recovery, to integrate into society via work and education, and to live vocationally productive and socially satisfying lives.

Clubhouse Philosophy: The Grand Avenue Club community offers powerful proof that adults who have experienced mental illness are capable of working, learning, and living in the community. Based on the Clubhouse Model of Psychiatric Rehabilitation, "Clubhouse" is an approach that is being used effectively by more than 300 similarly organized communities throughout the world. Via a pre-vocational work-ordered day, members run Grand Avenue Club while working closely with a small but dedicated staff. Members also access paid employment, achieve educational goals, acquire housing, and participate in the artistic and cultural life of Milwaukee. Grand Avenue Club has earned the highest accreditation status offered by Clubhouse International (www.clubhouse-intl.org), Clubhouse International, the training and accreditation headquarters for the global Clubhouse community.

The Four Rights of Membership:

Membership at Grand Avenue Club is entirely voluntary. Once someone becomes a member that person is guaranteed the right to:

- *A place to come*
- *A place to return after any absence*
- *Meaningful relationships*
- *Meaningful work*

- I continue to promote Waukesha County's *"Parents Who Host Lose the Most"* at Yo Cool Frozen Yogurt. The Department of Health Services has partnered with the Drug Free Action Alliance to sponsor this campaign to offer education to parents and communities about the safety and health risks of serving alcohol at underage teen parties. These adults can be criminally prosecuted for hosting teen alcohol parties. They can also be held liable for any injuries and property damage resulting from providing alcohol to teens.
- I have met with countless others, including jailers, sheriffs, EMTs, counselors, doctors, law enforcement, judges, and probation officers to find solutions to the problems facing us.
- I met with David Tetzlaff at Waukesha Social Services to discuss what can be done to improve the addiction situation facing our state and our country.
- I have spoken with Dr. Richard Davidson, Founder and Chair of The Center for Investigating Healthy Minds, University of Wisconsin, regarding addiction and the studies he is working on to help those afflicted. Dr. Davidson is best known for his groundbreaking work studying the brain and emotion. As a confidante and friend of the Dalai Lama, he is an expert and speaker, presenting on international stages such as the World Economic Forum, where he continues to serve on the Global Council on Mental Health. Dr. Davidson has also been named by *Time Magazine* in 2006, as one of "The 100 Most Influential People in the World."
- I spoke with Madeline Henry, Milwaukee Liaison to the Governor's office, to make changes supportive of

preventing drug abuse and to help those with addiction problems.

- I have contributed at The Addiction Resources Coalition meetings and continue to attend them as scheduled.
- I provided the Mequon Mayor, since 2013, Dan Abendroth, and Waukesha County Executive, Dan Vrakas (now retired) with information to assist with addiction problems and mental illness in their respective areas.
- I continue to work with the Waukesha Salvation Army giving help and assistance to those not able to get help elsewhere.
- I spoke with Renee Janusz, AODA (Alcohol and Other Drug Abuse) Case Manager since 2005 at Washington County Human Services, and have an open offer to speak at upcoming events regarding drinking, drugs, etc.
- I work with The ManKind Project, a group dedicated to help men with their problems, addictions and family issues. This is an outlet not readily found in society and is for the 21st Century. The ManKind Project is a nonprofit educational and training organization with over thirty years of proven success hosting life-changing and personal development programs for men. Supporting a global network of men's groups, The ManKind Project emphasizes the importance of leading lives of integrity, authenticity, and service.
- I have met with Judge William Brash and his wife Ruth. We discussed ways to create positive change regarding Wisconsin's addiction problem, mental illness and the

impact they both have on the legal system. William W. Brash III is a judge on the Wisconsin Court of Appeals, District 1. On October 28, 2015, he was appointed to the court by Wisconsin Governor, Scott Walker. In 2017, Judge Brash won the election to a full six-year term which ends on July 31, 2023.

- I began working on creating a non-profit mentor program for young people working their way into adulthood, as well as adults with addiction/legal problems, and life's problems. The program helps them to deal with the problems that lead them into addiction. The program is still in the works, part of the issue will be what we are able to do with the state resources. It is beginning to evolve into a plan for a standardized health program in the (hopefully elementary) schools, teaching young people about what they put in their bodies and why, how their minds work, what to do when they feel like they have problems, and who they can talk to. I do think the program will be more effective and reach more children if it is implemented through the schools, but it remains to be seen, and I continue to work on getting the details in order as it develops. Younger kids and teens in rural areas and the inner cities will need to be reached, which is why this program being implemented in the schools would be great; far more reaching than I could accomplish on my own.
- I have partnered with Shatterproof, a national non-profit organization dedicated to ending the horrible devastation and suffering addiction causes to families affected by it.
- I have met with Wisconsin Supreme Court Justice

Rebecca Bradley several times on addiction, and we are working together to improve the problem in our state. A Milwaukee native, Justice Bradley was elected to the Supreme Court in 2016 after being appointed by Governor Scott Walker in 2015.

- I was on the stage with Anderson Cooper of CNN at a Town Hall meeting in Milwaukee with the Republican Presidential Candidates for three hours on March 29th, 2016. I was not able to ask my questions on the air, but I was able to speak with the candidates privately about addiction, and Anderson Cooper asked if he could use me as an addiction resource.
- I have been on Fox News and CBS Sunday Morning shows talking about heroin, addiction, and the solutions I have for the problem.
- I received the Larry Stewart Humanitarian of the Year Award in January of 2016 from the Menomonee Falls Chamber of Commerce for my work on addiction.

I made this list because I wanted to show that there are many, many programs, events, and organizations that exist to combat the opioid and mental health issues, right in my own area. This list, of course, is not all inclusive, there are many charities, church groups, and government agencies that provide help as well. Organizations like these are in every community in my state, and throughout our country.

Anyone can show support at any level to combat these crises that affect all of us, in a variety of ways.

We can all do something.

EPILOGUE

As I finish writing this book, I face another challenge. I just found out that I have cancer. That was a shocking thing to hear. I don't know what the future holds for me, but I do know that whatever time I have left, I will devote whatever energy I have to continue fighting the fight against the addiction and mental health crises, to keep on trying to make an impact.

Knowing now that I have cancer, I can see a similarity between cancer and addiction. They are both major health crises in our country and the world, and there is not a person out there who is not affected by either of these (or both). We all know someone who is or has a friend or loved one who suffers; that is proof of what an epidemic addiction has become. It is *everywhere*. Everyone has issues, everyone needs help of some kind. We all need to encourage others to talk about what is happening in their lives and not hide it away until it hits the boiling point. Who knows the effect that will have on someone who is alone and facing demons, or death, or has thoughts of suicide or turning to substances to mask their pain? No person should bottle up the emotional pain of struggle. Be an angel to someone.

We can *all* do something. It doesn't matter what your station in life is. It can be something seemingly incidental like giving money to a cause. It can be helping a person or family who is struggling, or maybe volunteering. We don't necessarily see or may never know how we will impact others with actions we may consider trivial.

I think so often we don't consider what the other half is going through. I have perspective now, I was very lonely in my dark times. My whole life was turned upside down, and it was really out of control. I understand what people go through, things like I did and worse, and I have an entire new way of thinking. There are people whose families have disowned them, they've burned bridges with their friends, they don't have a base of support, they are in despair. How do they pull themselves back up when they don't have that? I don't know how I would have gotten my life back together without support. People do it, and it amazes me that they can. Somehow we have to find a way to build that support, not to coddle them, but find a safety net for those who try to do it the right way but just need some help.

If we only knew how we have touched so many people throughout our lives. When I am alone at night, and I start feeling down, I think about this book and the potential it has to impact people, and that gives me *hope*. I hope that people who know me and my story, or who read this, can take something positive away that will help them in the future; to be an example of how to see hope behind tragedy, to understand that a person with addiction or mental health issues is not lazy or beyond help and to show them comfort and compassion, to be able to talk with a friend with an addicted child and tell him/her that there is hope, and to work compassionately and lovingly to find the help that person needs…to be an angel in someone's midst.

I forever believe I have angels in my midst. I see the evidence all the time. I believe in God, but I don't think you even need to believe in Him to look at what I've gone through and say all those things are just coincidences. It could be argued that when I came up with the name "Dan" when I was at the funeral for the family whose son had died is just a coincidence, but it would be very difficult to wrap that into a statistical model.

People have helped me in so many ways. It is the only way I made it through my toughest times. I could never have made it through losing everything, being disconnected from my family, being homeless, broke, in jail, in detox, rehab, being completely alone with nothing. I needed help, and the angels in my midst surrounded me and helped me by giving me rides to work or my court hearings, sharing a meal, sharing a room, lifting me up in their prayers. If I didn't have that, I would be pretty dismal. The blessings I have from people who care enough to give me the help I need, give me hope; it means so much to me, and it is what keeps me going and inspires me to try to impact others in the same way.

Even now as I am being treated for my cancer, my doctor and I already have discussed new treatment methods if our current plan doesn't work. That may mean going to an out-of-network clinic like Mayo. I told him my insurance may not cover it, and that I am broke. He said this is not something to worry about, that he would work with that hospital to make sure that was not going to be an issue and I can get the treatment I need to fight this terrible disease. He is an angel in the midst.

I have people I have talked with, and families that I have worked with who stay in contact with me to give me updates on their family members who struggle with addiction, and tell me how grateful they are for the help I give them. It is very humbling to hear that, and I don't always feel I deserve those accolades; I just did what I could do. I use my base of knowledge and connections, and I always have my main goal in mind: I do not—CANNOT—want to see anyone go through losing a loved one like I did.

People have told me that I have moved the needle in my state for the fight against addiction. Countless friends and family have told me how my journey has helped them to realize how much they need to appreciate their lives and learn to live for today. Yes, I have been through a lot. But, for good or bad, what I have been through is my evolution into the person I am today.

I always thought I was a good person; good man, like-able, approachable; I know I am a better man today, most likely because I understand myself better and I have many people to thank for that. I am also happy. That is a very important step in my evolution, to be happy.

At the end of the day, if you look at your life and you have evolved on any level regardless of where you've come from, what you have, don't have, whatever, maybe that is the essence of having lived.

If this story helps you to realize what a blessing each day is and perhaps how you can better appreciate your life, your day, it will make my journey worth it. If you're an addict, my wish is it helps you realize what not to do, and what you need to do to make your life better; that there is hope.

I will never forget Shay as long as I'm alive. I will hold him in my heart forever. I will always love Nina and Harley, and cherish them, and never forget what blessings they are to me.

I'll leave you with one last note, and it is what I say at the end of every speech and presentation I make (including the radio program I did to honor Shay): Whoever is in your life, make sure to give them a hug and say, "I love you." Hug your children, hug your family until they ask you to stop…then hug them again.

You never know if that time will be the last time you ever talk to a son, a daughter, a mom or dad, a friend.

Don't pass up the chance.

- Alex

AFTERWORD

By Susan Rickun

On January 4, 2016 my nineteen year-old daughter woke me up at 1 a.m. to tell me she was a heroin addict. My first reaction was total denial. There was no anger...just shock, disbelief, and shame. She said she was going to stop. I thought, "Ok, it can't be that bad. Nobody will have to know."

Being a teen in the 70s, the only thing I knew about heroin addicts was that they were the "worst of the worst." Heroin addicts were pictured as deceased people in alleys with needles still stuck in their arms. Looking back, I can see how ridiculous my thinking was. I had zero understanding of what life for a heroin addict and their loved ones was like. I had no idea how powerful this drug could be.

I was fortunate enough to have a dear friend, Steve LaDue, jump into action and introduce me to his college roommate, Alex Hoffmann. I didn't know anything about Alex, other than he lost a son to a heroin overdose, and he wanted to talk to me to see if he could help. It's mind-boggling that this sweet man was able to push the horror of his loss to the side and become a powerful advocate for addicts and their families. Alex's strength is inspirational.

Alex is a smart, compassionate, and empathetic man who goes the extra mile for people. When I had no idea which way to turn, Alex gave me direction. When I had no idea who to contact, Alex gave me names. When I had no idea what to expect from my daughter, Alex prepared me for the ugliness. When I wanted to give up, Alex's words kept me moving forward. It was Alex who taught me to stay involved in my daughter's therapy and with her doctor visits. It was Alex who taught me never to give up hope. Alex was there to help with encouragement when my daughter relapsed. He was never judgmental, but instead, he was saddened because he had heard the word "relapse" all too often.

I'm happy to say Alex has continued to be by my side to celebrate my daughter's successes. She has been clean for 17 months. Heroin hell seems to be behind us. With Alex's guidance, my baby has been saved.

Parents need to understand that there is help out there. Parents need to put shame and humiliation aside, reach out to people, and NEVER give up hope.

I smiled while I read Alex's book. He is so humble, never wanting accolades even though his experiences are invaluable to parents of addicts. It was ironic to hear him referring to his angels throughout the book. Alex Hoffmann is one of MY angels, and for that, I am eternally grateful.

Harley, Shay, and Nina having fun together on a summer day. Good memories.

Shay in high school.

Nina, Harley, and Shay at Harley's high school graduation (top). They were inseparable.

Shay Hoffmann

December 22 1990 – July 1 2013

From Shay's memorial service.

Natalie Decker (above, right) of Eagle River, WI, the youngest female professional race car driver in the country. She and her team donated the space on the car to acknowledge all of the work I had been doing for families on the addiction crisis.

Here I am pictured with former President George W. Bush, and former United States Congressman Patrick Kennedy. Like me, both of these men have struggled with addiction, and are passionate about working on the causes of addiction and mental health. One is a Democrat, one is Republican, but party lines are irrelevant when it comes to fighting this crisis.

With the Honorable Senators from Wisconsin: Tammy Baldwin (top), and Ron Johnson (bottom). Both are passionate about fighting the opioid crisis, and are another example that this fight knows no party line.

With Govoner of Wisconsin, Scott Walker. I sincerely appreciate him taking time to meet with me on several occasions.

ABOUT THE CO-AUTHORS

Marla McKenna

Marla met Alex when his life was more like Heaven. It was the mid-1990s, and he was the "banker" and she was the marketing specialist at Universal Savings Bank and Payment Processing. He helped her acquire her first mortgage. Years and time passed, and their careers took them in different directions. She had no idea what had transpired during his lifetime.

A few years ago, they reconnected on social media. Marla contacted Alex with the hopes of partnering together on her first children's book, *Mom's Big Catch*, and giving back to the community. Little did they know then, they'd team up on a different book. But just as the title acknowledges, we have angels in our midst. God had a plan. Marla began to learn about Alex's life and that he wanted to piece his story together in a book. Marla introduced Alex to her publisher, who loved the idea. It's been quite the journey writing this book but it's finally here. It was like nothing Marla has ever worked on before during her writing career. The book is built on real, raw emotion, extreme heartbreak, loss and forgiveness with light touches of humor, and many blessings. It was a true gift for Marla to be part of this book project, and she is grateful for Alex's friendship and belief in her.

Marla is the author of several fun and inspiring children's books and partial proceeds from these books benefit the Linda Blair WorldHeart Foundation, with special thanks to Rick Springfield for matching her donations. *Our Last Day in Heaven* is a new chapter in Marla's life.

Marla McKenna's passion for writing and sharing a positive message with children comes to life in all of her books. She loves visiting schools and teaching the importance of patience, positivity, perseverance and giving back. Inspired by her daughters, Julia and Ashley, Marla continues to write books while living in Wisconsin with her family. For more information on Marla's work, please visit marlamckenna.com

Alex, thank you for your courage and strength as we journeyed through this book together. I cried, and then I cried again but we smiled a bit too. I believe *Our Last Day in Heaven* has the power to heal, teach and inspire, and you are a true inspiration. Don't ever give up my friend, you have more good work to do!

- Marla

Michael Nicloy

Michael is the owner and publisher of Nico 11 Publishing & Design. He lives in Mukwonago, Wisconsin with his wife, Angela, and their two sons, Liam T. MK, and Shayden M.K.

Michael is grateful to Alex for the opportunity to be a part of sharing his story. The world needs to know that there is hope in the face of tragedy, and that there are warriors in the fight against opioid addiction. The mantra Alex is always repeating is that "we can all do something," and Alex wants to spread all of those messages with this book.

Alex, Michael, and Marla want to extend their deepest gratitude to Wisconsin Attorney General Brad Schimel, U.S. Senator (Wisconsin) Ron Johnson, Wisconsin Representative John Nygren, Attorney Michael Rowgowski, Waukesha County Executive Paul Farrow, and Susan Rickun for their contributions not only to this book, for listineng to and working with Alex, a well as in their jobs and daily lives fighting the fight against opioid crisis. These people, when asked for their testimonials, all responded the same: "Anything I can do for Alex Hoffmann."

That is a true testament to Alex the person, and especially Alex the warrior.

Alex, I know it wasn't easy to recount the horror of losing your Shay for this book, but good will come of it. I count you as a dear friend, and you know I have your back—ALWAYS. Much love, Alex.

Stay strong. Fight on!

- Mike

SOURCES

1 www.cdc.gov/drugoverdose/epidemic

2 Fox6Now.com 14 Dec 2017

3 Bureau of Justice Statistics, Annual Probation Survey, Annual Parole Survey, Annual Survey of Jails, Census of Jail Inmates, and National Prisoner Statistics Program, 1980-2015. Date 2/24/2017.

4 Bureau of Justice Statistics, "Drug Offenders in Federal Prison: Estimates of Characteristics Based on Linked Data". Date October, 2015. A male federal prisoner costs at least $30,000 per year to incarcerate, and females actually cost more.

5 Treating and diverting: *Heroin Task Force reports on the status of addictions, recovery*
By Melanie Boyung - News Graphic Staff
Feb. 13, 2018
http://www.gmtoday.com/content/m_magazine/2014/May/m_052014_48.asp

6 Fortune.com "Walgreens Is Now Selling a Drug That Can Reverse Opioid Overdoses" 10/26/2017 Lisa Marie Segarra

7 Time.com (Time Magazine online) Alice Park, 26 October, 2017

8 Fox6now.com

9 "This is an epidemic:" Milwaukee Co. receives $2.6M+ in grants to combat opioid abuse, addiction; fox6now.com 27 Nov, 2017

Fox6 Milwaukee (WITI) is presenting an excellent ongoing series on the opiod crisis on their website called "Dose of Reality." Visit: www.fox6now.com/category/dose-of-reality/

Made in the USA
San Bernardino, CA
27 July 2018